ERIN GO GRAY!

⇥ AN IRISH REBEL TRILOGY ⇤

ED GLEESON

MAPS BY RICHARD DAY

The Lewis Library, Vincennes University
Vincennes, Indiana

GUILD PRESS OF INDIANA
Carmel, Indiana

Printed in the United States of America

Library of Congress Number
97-78019

ISBN 1-57860-017-0 (HARDBACK)
ISBN 1-57860-018-9 (PAPERBACK)

OTHER BOOKS BY ED GLEESON

Rebel Sons of Erin: A Civil War Unit History of the Tenth Tennessee Infantry Regiment (Irish) Confederate States Volunteers

Illinois Rebels: A Civil War Unit History of G Company Fifteenth Tennessee Regiment Volunteer Infantry

CONTENTS

MAPS

PHOTOGRAPHS

INTRODUCTION

AN EXAMINATION OF CONFEDERATE MUSTER ROLLS REVEALS that no fewer than twenty thousand foreign-born Irishmen but no more than twenty-five thousand of these native Hibernians served the South in some capacity during the War Between the States. Whatever the exact numbers, they pale in comparison to the approximately 275,000 Irish immigrants in Union service. Traditionally the problem has been that even the most avid of WBTS readers have assumed, for reasons not always clear, that General Pat Cleburne was the only Irishman in the Provisional Army of the Confederate States.

In spite of the fact that Cleburne was, without question, the greatest of all the Irish Rebels, his place of birth, as listed on the muster rolls, was hardly unique. During the 1990s an awareness of the contributions made by many other gray-clad Irishmen has moderately increased. My first book, *Rebel Sons of Erin*, a regimental history of the Tenth Tennessee Infantry, helped to fill some of the void. Although it still remains a somewhat obscure subject, Irish Rebeldom has finally caught the attention of contemporary buffs, as least from Nashville to Boston.

My true mission in life, that is, to lead a massive Irish Confederate full frontal assault across Federally occupied America, was temporarily sidetracked by the appearance of my second book, *Illinois Rebels*, a slight aberration that resulted from my fascination with Confederate troops residing in the southernmost counties of my home state. Now back on course, my attack against the sensitivities of political correctness resumes with *Erin Go Gray!*, a title that has been attached to this collection of Irish Rebel essays by my publisher.

Along with the thousands of Irish immigrants who fought for the Southern Confederacy, there were tens of thousands of American-born sons of Irish immigrants who fought along side them, including father and son combinations like my ancestors, John and Michael Condon of Hawkins County, Tennessee. Both groups are represented here. General Finegan and many of the Tennessee troops were immigrants, while Father Ryan and many more of the Tennessee troops were sons of immigrants. For all of these Confederate champions of Irish America, let freedom ring!

Ed Gleeson
Oak Lawn, Illinois
St. Patrick's Day
Monday, March 17, 1997

ON YE GO, BRAVE LADS

GENERAL JOSEPH FINEGAN

GENERAL JOSEPH FINEGAN

THERE WERE SIX IRISH-BORN GENERALS in Confederate service. One was Patrick R. Cleburne. The other five weren't. This essay is about one of the Southern Irish generals who wasn't Cleburne. His name was Joseph Finegan, not Finnegan. Like Cleburne, Finegan wasn't Catholic, charming, or witty. And he never led green-flag Irish troops in battle. In fact both Irish generals, on several occasions, led their commands against green-flag Irish troops in battle. Also like Cleburne, Finegan was highly organized, courageous in battle, and completely devoted to the Southern cause. Here the comparison ends dramatically. Unlike Cleburne, Finegan was strictly a political appointee. Although Joseph Finegan understood the fundamental tactics of military deployment, his use of troops in battle was consistently over-aggressive to the point of reckless incompetency. Enigmatic, controversial, and one of the most unloved general officers of the Confederacy, "Old Barney" remains just as obscure today as he did the day he died 112 years ago.

"Finegan, me bye, ye know ye are yur mither's darlin'," was how the Irishman referred to himself with a twinkle in his eye. Joseph Finegan was born November 17, 1814, at Clones, County Monaghan, Ireland, and emigrated to the east coast of Florida in 1835 at the age of twenty. In 1837 the handsome young Irishman married a beautiful and wealthy widow, Rebecca Travers, who had three daughters by a first marriage. He was twenty-two; she was twenty-five. The Finegans subsequently had three children of their own, two sons and a daughter. The oldest child, Joseph Rutledge Finegan, was named after the Episcopal bishop of Florida. (In October of 1862 Rutledge would be commissioned a first lieutenant and appointed assistant adjutant to his father.) In 1851 the family moved from the Atlantic Ocean coastal town of St. Augustine north to the coastal town of Jacksonville, where Joseph used Rebecca's money to purchase a lumber mill and a mercantile business. Making a considerable profit in four years, the Finegans moved north again to the next beach town on the coastal map—Fernandina (modern city of Fernandina Beach) on Amelia's Island in the extreme northeastern tip of Florida below Brunswick, Georgia.

Here the Irishman practiced law and met David L. Yulee, a prominent businessman and future U.S. senator. The two friends combined resources and made a small fortune constructing and operating the Florida Railroad Company with lines between the Atlantic coast and the Gulf coast, linking northern Florida with the western Southern states.[1]

The Finegan plantation, just outside of Fernandina, was described as "one of the finest in the vicinity, a three-storied white frame structure with sprawling piazzas in front and rear, surrounded by trees of orange and wild olives and approached by a long lane lined with semi-tropical vegetation and with slaves all around the place." Born and raised in the Anglican Church of Ireland, Joseph Finegan sent all six of his children to private schools. By 1860 the forty-five-year-old Irishman had achieved the American dream. Described as "jovial and hearty," he was a wealthy and influential gentleman, firmly entrenched in his belief and devotion to God, country, family, plantation and the traditional Southern philosophy of life. In two years it would all be gone with the wind. Without a knowledge of Finegan's background, it is impossible to understand the grim, humorless, unyielding, uncompromising Confederate officer, under whose controversial leadership captured black Union soldiers would later be slaughtered on battlefields in both Florida and Virginia.[2]

Strongly pro-slavery and pro-secession, Old Barney, the Southern Democratic politician, represented Nassau County during the state convention that gathered in December of 1860 at the Florida capital city of Tallahassee. Nassau, including Amelia's Island, was an area inhabited mostly by Georgia and South Carolina natives. On January 10, 1861, the convention pulled Florida out of the Federal Union by a vote of 62 to 7, with Finegan voting with the majority. After passage of the Ordinance of Secession, Florida Governor Madison Starke Perry appointed Representative Finegan as director of state military affairs. The position was an administrative office, not military in nature.[3]

Director Finegan used his personal efficiency and sound business sense to recruit and organize volunteer companies for both state militia and Confederate service. The training of all units was left to the elected officers. The task of the Irishman was formidable. Florida was, by far, the least populated of the Southern states, a spacious and mostly unoccupied land of beaches, palm trees, swamps, and alligators. The 1860 census reported a state population of about 140,000 men, women, and children, half white and half black, most of whom lived in the upper part of the state. Most of the blacks were slaves and many of the white men were young boys, old men, and wealthy planters, all exempt from military service. Also, a sizable minority of Floridians were pro-Union. On more than one occasion Director Finegan, through newspaper ads, had to appeal to pro-Confederate citizens for weapons to arm his volunteers.[4]

Between early 1861 and early 1862 Barney Finegan worked a logistics miracle by forming Florida companies from 4,827 armed volunteers, who were then divided into two serviceable brigades, each of three regiments. One brigade, under Brigadier General Edward A. Perry, was sent to the Army of Northern Virginia on the eastern front. The other, under Brigadier General Jesse J. Finley, was sent to the Army of Tennessee on the western front, leaving only a few hundred militiamen behind to defend Florida. Several influential officers, including Generals Robert E. Lee and P. G. T. Beauregard, noted and praised the organizational skills of Florida military director Joseph Finegan. Unfortunately for Florida Governor John Milton (who had succeeded M. S. Perry) and Director Finegan, the Confederate War Department in Richmond showed little interest in defending Florida, most of which was considered useless to the war effort. Fortunately for Milton and Finegan, the Union War Department in Washington City demonstrated the same lack of interest in Florida real estate. The Federals were, however, eager to protect their Atlantic Fleet blockading the eastern coast against Confederate blockade runners.[5]

On November 7, 1861, Admiral Samuel F. DuPont captured two Confederate forts guarding the entrance to Port Royal Sound on the coast of South Carolina, just two hundred miles north of the Florida coast. With no resistance from the small Confederate Navy, DuPont sailed south to capture Fort Clinch near Fernandina on Amelia's Island. Brigadier General James H. Trapier, commanding the District of Middle and East Florida in the Confederate Department of South

Carolina, Georgia, and Florida had a few hundred garrison troops from the Fourth Florida Infantry Battalion at the fort and along the north Florida coast. When DuPont's transports landed infantry to secure the harbors at Fernandina, Jacksonville, and St. Augustine in February of 1862, Trapier was forced to evacuate the coastal region without a fight and fall back into the interior. There was a military supply warehouse in Jacksonville which Trapier ordered destroyed early in March, so that the Federals would not gain possession. In the process of carrying out the order, the Florida Confederates somehow managed to accidentally burn the state's largest town (population 1,333) nearly to the ground, causing many pro-Confederate Jacksonville citizens to riot against their own troops, while converting to the Union cause. After securing the Florida coast from blockade runners the Union Army and Navy, showing no interest in Florida's interior, withdrew and sailed back north. During this brief Federal occupation, the Finegan plantation was looted and the Irishman's slaves were set free.[6]

General Trapier was humiliated by the accidental burning of Jacksonville; his military reputation, like much of the town, was ruined. Replacing Trapier as commanding officer of the District of Middle and East Florida was Joseph Finegan himself, who had been raving at district headquarters about his own home's being left unprotected. The appointment was made by President Jefferson Davis at the request of Senator Yulee and over the objection of Governor Milton, who considered Finegan to be an excellent organizer but even less qualified to command troops than Trapier. Commissioned a brigadier general of volunteers in the regular Confederate Army on April 8, 1862, the forty-seven-year-old Irishman was assigned to head all state of Florida "forces" consisting of exactly six infantry companies, six cavalry companies, and two artillery companies. (The rank of brigadier was the only one he ever held. The highness of the rank was due to the fact that Davis was obligated to name a certain number of general officers from each state.)[7]

General Finegan's superior was Major General John C. Pemberton, the Philadelphia Quaker who commanded the Department of South Carolina, Georgia, and Florida. Giving his new subordinate something useful to do, Pemberton ordered Finegan to construct two forts. One garrison was to be established on the Apalachicola River, which empties into the Gulf of Mexico west and south of Tallahassee. The other garrison was to be established on the St. John's River, which empties into the Atlantic Ocean just above Jacksonville. The purpose of the west coast fortification was to protect the state capital from Federal raids out of Alabama or Georgia. The purpose of the east coast fortification was to protect the remaining blockade runners.[8]

Establishing his headquarters in the interior at Lake City between Tallahassee and Jacksonville, the commanding general of all Florida put his fourteen companies to good use. With no battles to fight, the Irishman worked another logistics miracle. The battery he constructed at Alum Bluff rose a hundred feet above the Apalachicola, directly west of Tallahassee, blocking any Federal advance on the river from Georgia or Alabama to the gulf. Finegan's western fort had seven guns, four of which were heavy, with a garrison of about ninety dismounted cavalrymen.[9]

The battery constructed by the Irishman at St. John's Bluff was located just five miles from the Federal port of Mayport Mills in an excellent position to dispute the passage of enemy gunboats. Finegan's eastern fort had eight heavy guns and a garrison consisting of Lieutenant Colonel Charles F. Hopkins' First Florida Special Battalion, whose task was to support Major Theodore Brevard's gun crew. When some of DuPont's gunboats were harassed in September by Finegan's shells, the admiral determined to capture the pesky battery on the St. John's. To the dismay of the Florida troops it was soon discovered that their commanding general had made a considerable mistake in judgment. The Irishman had secured St. John's Bluff against a navy river attack but had not anticipated an army infantry landing. Consequently Hopkins and Brevard were provided with only a few rounds of small arms ammunition.[10]

On September 30, 1862, Hopkins at St. John's Bluff wired Finegan at Lake City with an intelligence report that had located Federal troop transports off the South Carolina coast, sailing south. Realizing his mistake too late, Finegan wired departmental headquarters at

Charleston with an urgent request for two properly armed Georgia regiments to be dispatched immediately from Savannah. General Beauregard, who had replaced General Pemberton as commanding general of the Department of South Carolina, Georgia, and Florida, sent one regiment but the Georgians arrived too late to reinforce the Floridians.[11]

On October 2, Irish-American Brigadier General John M. Brannon disembarked from DuPont's boats with a small brigade of 1,573 Union infantrymen from the Seventh Connecticut and Forty-Seventh Pennsylvania regiments, and marched his command inland from Mayport Mills to St. John's Bluff. Acting with extreme caution, Hopkins evacuated his command of better than 600 effectives without any resistance. Even worse he failed to spike the guns. The absurd affair ended when the Federals packed the eight heavy guns on their boats and sailed away with them. Before departing the Florida coast, the Northerners again occupied and quickly abandoned the town of Jacksonville, demonstrating a consistent disregard for the state's interior. The loss of the recently constructed battery at St. John's Bluff without a fight was equally as embarrassing to the Florida Confederates as the accidental burning of the town the previous spring. Even though Finegan and Hopkins both made mistakes that contributed to the latest humiliation, both men bitterly blamed each other in a dispute that lasted for the rest of their lives. In a letter to Senator Yulee, General Finegan explained his position: "I had seven hundred men in and around the battery. Sufficient—if they had stood their ground— to hold the place. It was an unfortunate affair and reflects little credit on the officer in command."[12]

Following the fiasco at St. John's Bluff below Jacksonville, the Richmond War Department was reluctantly forced to admit the impossibility of defending the entire state of Florida with a single command of fourteen companies. Within the Department of South Carolina, Georgia, and Florida, Finegan's former District of Middle and East Florida was split in half with the Irishman commanding the District of East Florida (northern Florida from the gulf to the ocean) and with Brigadier General Howell Cobb, a middle-aged Georgia politician, commanding the District of Middle Florida (central Florida

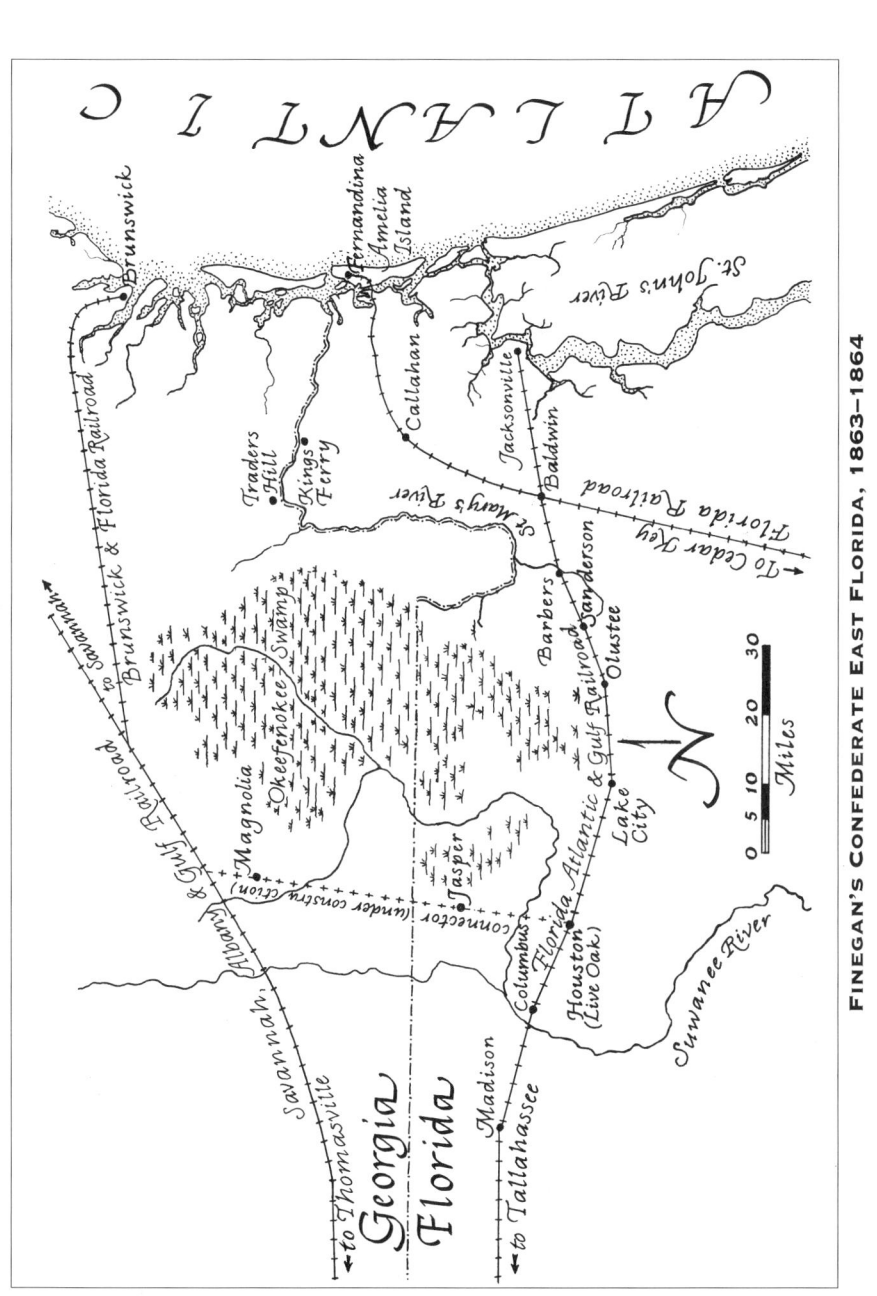

FINEGAN'S CONFEDERATE EAST FLORIDA, 1863–1864

from the gulf to the ocean). Since the bottom third of the state was inhabited mainly by alligators, Richmond deemed it unnecessary to organize a "District of South Florida."[13]

In reality the 'gators were in a better position to dispute future
Federal invasions than Generals Cobb or Finegan. Instead of sending
reinforcements to the two new districts, the War Department merely
divided the fourteen companies of garrison forces between Cobb and
Finegan, with each command being supplemented with Florida militiamen. Old Barney was left to defend the two most important towns
in the state—Tallahassee and Jacksonville—with less than his original
command. Meanwhile, Presidents Abraham Lincoln and Jefferson
Davis continued to share at least one thing in common—a total lack
of interest in Florida.[14]

Early in the year of 1863, as the town of Jacksonville was beginning to rebuild, the Federals made another surprise visit. This time
their mission was to free slaves in the area and recruit them into the
Union Army. The St. Mary's River empties into the ocean above
Fernandina. There were plantations all along the river. Federal transports sailed up the St. Mary's carrying two army regiments—the First
and Second U.S. South Carolina (Colored) under Colonels Thomas
W. Higginson and James Montgomery. These black troops consisted
mostly of enlisted men who were former slaves. After freeing the remaining slaves on the river and recruiting some of them into Federal
service, the invaders sacked Joseph Finegan's abandoned plantation for
the second time in six months, causing the Irishman to become deeply
bitter about the behavior of black enemy troops. (Like most plantation
owners Finegan had always feared a "slave revolt" like Nate Turner's
or the one that occurred in 1803 when the French were thrown out of
Haiti.) The two black regiments sailed down to Jacksonville on March
3 to gather more recruits and were joined a week later by two white
regiments—the Sixth Connecticut and the Eighth Maine. With only
a few companies of garrison troops at his disposal there was not a great
deal that Finegan could do about this unhappy situation, except to
angrily curse the "abolitionists" and "contrabands."[15]

While the white officers and black enlisted men of the First and
Second U.S. South Carolina regiments searched for more recruits, the

two regiments of white New Englanders advanced to the western out-skirts of Jacksonville, established an improvised river battery and, along with some of their gunboats, kept Finegan busy by firing some shells in his direction. Not sure about enemy intentions, the Irishman sent a request for reinforcements to Cobb, and in turn received a few cavalrymen and a 32-pounder cannon.[16]

With considerable difficulty General Finegan's engineers had the big rifled gun mounted onto a railroad flatcar on the tracks of the Florida, Atlantic, and Gulf Central Railroad west of Jacksonville. Shortly before midnight of March 24, the Irish commander ordered Captain Thomas E. Buckman to move the railroad gun to within a mile and a half of town. On the following morning at 3:30, Private Francis C. Sollee fired seven shots toward the enemy battery, six of which missed everything, one of which demolished an abandoned cabin. With no infantry support, the big gun was forced back into the interior, as ten companies of New Englanders quickly advanced three miles west of Jacksonville where they tore up the track, preventing any further use of Finegan's moving artillery. Neither side reported any casualties during the odd "Battle of the Railroad Gun."[17]

For the third time in the period of one year the Northerners had occupied Jacksonville, accomplished their mission, demonstrated no interest in the Florida interior, and evacuated the place. Before the men of the four Federal regiments boarded their transports on March 28, some of them looted and burnt what little was left of the town, in-cluding St. John's Catholic Church, the parish community of many of Finegan's fellow Irishmen. Finegan vehemently blamed the black sol-diers only; but in fact, both white and black troops participated in the wanton destruction. Pro-Union citizens who had once been pro-Con-federate citizens switched back to their original partisanship and began to rebuild their town once again. There would be no more military activity in Florida for another year. As if on an annual schedule the Northerners would return to Jacksonville in February of 1864. They would then make the one huge mistake that they had previously avoided in the Sunshine State. Foolishly, they would invade the inte-rior, where a vengeful Irish general would be waiting for them amidst the swamps and alligators.[18]

The critical back-to-back Union successes of July 3–4, 1863, at Gettysburg and Vicksburg, indicated that an end to the war might be in sight. On September 19–20, however, the Confederate Army of Tennessee destroyed one-third of the Union Army of the Cumberland during a decisive Southern victory in northern Georgia just south of Chattanooga, Tennessee along the West Chickamauga Creek. Instead of anticipating an early resolution to the conflict, Federal authorities were called upon to plan a massive two-pronged invasion of the South for the spring of 1864, with Major General William T. Sherman marching into Georgia with an army group of three armies and Lieutenant General U. S. Grant marching into Virginia with another army group of three armies. Eighteen sixty-four was also going to be an election year, and the bloody war was becoming increasingly unpopular in the North. President Lincoln wanted to be re-elected, while his own treasury secretary, Salmon P. Chase, wanted to bump Lincoln off the Republican ticket. In the midst of the greatest calamity in American history, supporters of both Lincoln and Chase schemed to invade Florida, establish a Union-loyal state government, and then win Florida's three electoral votes at the National Convention![19]

Over the strenuous objections of the Washington City War Department, which correctly considered the interior of Florida to be strategically worthless, the politicians settled on four objectives for a Florida campaign: 1) Procure an outlet for the products of the state. 2) Cut off the enemy's source of commissary supplies, especially beef. 3) Secure more recruits for colored regiments. 4) Inaugurate measures for the restoration of Florida to allegiance in accordance with the desire of the President. Responsibility for the "Federal Expeditionary Force" fell to Major General Quincy Adams Gillmore, commanding the Union Department of the South, with headquarters at Hilton Head Island, South Carolina. Under a Navy escort provided by Admiral J. A. Dahlgren, General Gillmore's transports landed at Jacksonville on February 7, 1864, carrying a detached army corps of two divisions of five brigades under the field command of Brigadier General Truman Seymour. It was to be the fourth and last Federal occupation of the beleaguered Florida coastal town.[20]

The Federal invading force consisted of thirteen infantry regiments (five of which consisted of black soldiers), one cavalry regiment, one cavalry battalion and four artillery batteries, for a total of slightly more than 7,000 officers and men. On the same day that the landings began, Confederate scouts reported the bad news to General Finegan at Lake City. At that time the Irishman had a command of four small battalions scattered all over the District of East Florida. The First, Second, and Sixth Florida Infantry Battalions had about 490 men among them, while the Second Florida Cavalry Battalion had only about 110 men, a total of some 600 effectives to oppose the 7,000 Federals. (The First Cavalry Battalion and the Fourth Infantry Battalion were on service in the District of Middle Florida.)[21]

Also on that same day, Finegan wired Beauregard for heavy reinforcements. Receiving the telegram at Charleston on the next day, the Louisianian ordered Brigadier General Alfred H. Colquitt of Georgia to march south from Savannah and report to Finegan at Lake City with eight infantry regiments, one cavalry regiment, and three artillery batteries, all from Georgia, mostly experienced combat veterans. On February 8, as Beauregard was organizing reinforcements for Finegan, Seymour ordered his cavalry brigade of one regiment and one battalion under Colonel Guy V. Henry to ride west and capture lightly defended Camp Finegan, a few miles west of Jacksonville. During the next five days Finegan skillfully deployed individual companies in front of Henry to slow him down before withdrawing his meager Florida Confederate forces.[22]

Generals Gillmore and Seymour met at Barber's Plantation on the west tributary of the St. Mary's River, between Jacksonville and Lake City, on February 13. The Northern generals agreed that their mission had been accomplished, especially in regards to securing the Jacksonville area for the purpose of forming a Union-loyal state government to oppose the Confederate state government at Tallahassee. Sailing back up to his departmental headquarters at Hilton Head, Gillmore left Seymour behind to entrench in a defensible position west of Jacksonville, recruit more ex-slaves, gather up livestock, and ship supplies north. An ambitious Truman Seymour was not, however, feeling good about his own career. Here he was in the middle of no man's land rounding up cattle while other officers won glory and fame on the major fronts. After sitting around dejected for a few more days, Seymour determined to become a hero. Disregarding Gillmore's instructions, the Federal field commander decided to advance his troops westward completely across the width of Florida with the intent of capturing Tallahassee. Ironically, if Seymour had reacted quickly he would have easily swept Finegan's garrison forces into the underbrush. Good fortune smiled on the Irishman. Seymour moved out on February 19, the very day after the final Confederate reinforcements arrived by train from Georgia.[23]

Seymour had been receiving vague scouting reports about an enemy buildup around Lake City. Failing to send reconnaissance patrols that far west, he had no idea about how many Southerners were in the interior or who commanded them. As a result the Union commander committed another huge error in judgment and left five of his thirteen infantry regiments in reserve on the coast between Fernandina and Jacksonville. The remaining units were divided into four small brigades. In addition to Henry's cavalry brigade of one regiment and one battalion there were three undersized infantry brigades. The racially mixed First Brigade, commanded by Colonel Joseph R. Hawley, consisted of the Seventh Connecticut, the Seventh New Hampshire, and the Eighth United States (Colored). The all-white Second Brigade, commanded by Colonel William B. Barton, consisted of the Forty-Seventh, Forty-Eighth and One-Hundred-Fifteenth New York regiments. The all-black Third Brigade, commanded by Colonel James Montgomery, consisted of the First U.S. North Carolina (Colored) and the Fifty-Fourth Massachusetts (Colored), the latter unit having earned a good combat record the previous July at Battery Wagner. General Seymour also had four batteries of artillery with sixteen guns.[24]

General Finegan wisely entrenched in an excellent position thirteen miles east of Lake City at the Railroad Station of Olustee near a 'gator-infested marsh known as Ocean Pond. Unlike his Northern opponent, the Irishman left only one unit in reserve—the First Florida Infantry Battalion. He logically divided the rest of his command into a division of three brigades. The First Brigade, under Colquitt, was formed from the Sixth, Nineteenth, Twenty-Third, Twenty-Seventh, and Twenty-Eighth Georgia Infantry regiments, plus the Sixth Florida Infantry Battalion. The Second Brigade, under youthful Colonel George P. Harrison, was formed from the First, Thirty-Second, and Sixty-Fourth Georgia Infantry regiments, plus the Second Florida Infantry Battalion. The Third Brigade, under Colonel Caraway Smith, was (like the Federal cavalry brigade) formed from the only two available cavalry units—the Fourth Georgia Cavalry regiment and the Second Florida Cavalry Battalion. Finegan also had three batteries of artillery with twelve guns. Because of the differences in reserve strength, both sides went into battle with almost exactly the same number of effectives—fifty-one hundred officers and men.[25]

Incorrectly assuming that he would easily oust the Southerners from Lake City on February 21, General Seymour advanced his infantry on Sunday morning, February 20, with the Seventh Connecticut in the lead. At about 2 P.M. Colonel Henry's troopers and Colonel Hawley's troops ran into General Finegan's pickets three miles east of the main Confederate works at Ocean Pond. At the same time that Seymour launched his piecemeal assault, Finegan rushed combat-experienced elements of General Colquitt's brigade forward to meet Hawley's New Englanders. During the four hour confrontation that followed, Finegan remained at the breastworks near Ocean Pond, acting as his own staff officer, while Colquitt commanded the troops in the field. In regards to the timing of troop movements that afternoon, Finegan was consistently very good, very lucky, or both, while Seymour was very bad, very unlucky, or both.[26]

The Seventh Connecticut, armed with inadequate skirmish-line weapons, withdrew, while conflicting orders caused the Seventh New Hampshire to break in confusion. A complete rout of Hawley's brigade was avoided when the inexperienced black South Carolinians of the Eighth United States (Colored) came up and temporarily held the Union line. When Colquitt's advance was momentarily checked by Hawley's blacks, the Georgian sent a message back west to Finegan for reinforcements. The Irishman anticipated the request and the other units of Colquitt's brigade, including the Sixth Florida Battalion, arrived on the field almost immediately after the request. The white Georgians and Floridians charged and the black South Carolinians fell back at first in good order and then in panic. Seymour continued to deploy one regiment at a time, giving the Confederates a considerable numerical advantage throughout the action. When the lead companies of Colonel Barton's white New Yorkers assaulted the battle line of Colquitt's brigade, Finegan countered with Colonel Harrison's brigade, including the Second Florida Battalion. Colquitt and Harrison counterassaulted with their force of eight Georgia regiments and two Florida battalions, pushing Barton's three New York regiments further east into the woods and swamps. The Confederate offensive movement stalled at four when small arms ammunition began to run low.[27]

General Finegan also anticipated the ammunition shortage. With some ingenuity he had spent the previous two hours gathering up all of the ammunition that could be found in the Olustee area. Cartridge boxes were loaded onto train box cars and arrived at the front at almost the exact same time that the Southerners had fired their last round. Colquitt and Harrison were then able to drive the last companies of Hawley and Barton off the field. With most of his white New Englanders, white New Yorkers, and black South Carolinians already out of the fight, Seymour advanced the last two available regiments of his division—Colonel Montgomery's First U.S. North Carolina (Colored) and Fifty-Fourth Massachusetts (Colored).[28]

As the remnant of Hawley and Barton retreated and as the lead companies of Montgomery advanced, Finegan personally led his only reserve unit, the First Florida Battalion, onto the western end of the battlefield. On the east end of the field, the two fresh black regiments came up on the Union left (south end of Seymour's unstable line) and pushed some of the Georgians and Floridians back west to their skirmish line. When Finegan threw the First Florida Battalion into the brawl, the First U.S. North Carolina, consisting of both free blacks and ex-slaves, was battered back east into the woods. The Fifty-Fourth Massachusetts, consisting almost exclusively of free black veterans from Boston and Philadelphia, held its position without much help from other Federal troops, white or black.[29]

Admitting defeat shortly after six, Seymour withdrew from the field and retreated his division east toward the coast, with the blacks of the Fifty-Fourth Massachusetts serving as rear guards for the retirement. Ocean Pond, or Olustee Station, the only major Civil War battle fought in Florida, had resulted in an overwhelming Southern victory, with Finegan and his men receiving the official thanks of the Confederate Congress. The Federals left Jacksonville for the fourth time and never returned. Tallahassee remained the only Confederate state capital east of the Mississippi River never to fall into enemy hands. General Seymour had foolishly invaded the swamps and 'gators of Florida's interior and failed miserably. He was outmaneuvered by General Finegan and outfought by General Colquitt. The magnitude of the defeat overshadowed an especially fine performance by black Union troops. The bizarre invasion cost the Federals 203 killed, 1,152 wounded, and 506 captured or missing for a total of 1,861 losses, a staggering thirty-seven percent of those engaged, one of the highest casualty rates of any battle in American history. The Confederates had 93 killed and 841 wounded for total losses of 934 or eighteen percent of those engaged.[30]

Some nineteenth-century observers interpreted Finegan's lack of presence on the Ocean Pond battlefield as a sign of physical cowardice. This presumption cannot be supported by fact. On later Virginia battlefields the Irishman consistently demonstrated more personal valor than wisdom. Finegan's problem was a lack of experience, not a lack of courage. Two years of garrison duty did not prepare him for war on a large scale. Personal shortcomings and the lack of a military background led the Irish general to make two serious blunders following his victory in the swamps.

First, Finegan failed to aggressively pursue the shattered Federal command, allowing a badly beaten foe to get away. Seymour's performance in battle was poor, but he had at least enough common sense to quickly get his survivors back to Jacksonville and out of Florida. Just as he had blamed Colonel Hopkins for the problem at St. John's Bluff, Finegan blamed Colonel Caraway Smith, his cavalry commander, for letting the Northerners escape at Olustee. In his report to departmental headquarters in Charleston the Irishman made his case:

During the continuance of the battle, also after the enemy had given way, I sent repeated orders to Colonel Smith, commanding cavalry, to press the enemy on his flanks and to continue in the pursuit. But through some misapprehension these orders failed to be executed by him, and only two small companies on the left, and these but a short distance, followed the enemy.

Smith denied that he received the "repeated orders." A lack of any dispatches from Finegan to Smith supports Smith's version of the events. Beauregard, knowing full well that the commanding general was responsible for all field operations, did not accept Finegan's excuse. Smith, like Hopkins before him, was later exonerated from all official charges.[31]

Second, although there is no evidence that the Irishman ordered captured black soldiers to be abused, there is substantial evidence that he knowingly allowed abuse to take place. Several negative incidents involving captured black Federals occurred throughout the War Between the States. Ocean Pond was, however, the only place where both white officers commanding black regiments as well as their black enlisted men were mistreated. Eyewitness accounts on both sides verify this. In striking contrast, officers and men from white regiments were treated well. Finegan's bitterness about the loss of his own plantation and the possibility of his own former slaves fighting against him contributed to the hostility. Colonel Charles W. Fribley, the young white officer who commanded the Fifty-Fourth Massachusetts, was killed while courageously defending his position. Under a flag of truce after the battle, Seymour requested reasonably that the body be sent forward to Union lines. Finegan responded that the body could not be found. The Irishman confided to Yulee that he never even looked for the remains of the "abolitionist." (Finegan had the annoying habit of referring to all white Northerners as abolitionists. In point of fact, Colonel Montgomery *was* an abolitionist; Colonel Fribley and the vast majority of white Union soldiers were not.) In the context of those desperate times General Finegan's attitudes and conduct must be understood but not condoned.[32]

In spite of his ineffective pursuit and mistreatment of prisoners of war, Joseph Finegan had won an emotionally important Southern victory at a critical period of time. His efforts were praised by the pro-

Confederate Florida press, and he was given hero status by his business partner, David Yulee. While Finegan remained in the District of East Florida with his garrison forces, Colquitt, Harrison, and the Georgia troops were sent to the Virginia front. On May 4, 1864, Lieutenant General U. S. Grant launched a huge offensive into northern Virginia for the purpose of capturing the Confederate capital at Richmond. What resulted were the bloody first two battles of the Overland Campaign—Wilderness and Spotsylvania Courthouse. Although General Robert E. Lee successfully blocked Grant's attempt to "slide his way left" into Richmond, the Army of Northern Virginia suffered heavy casualties. Edward Perry's Florida brigade, which Finegan had helped to organize, consisted of the Second, Fifth, and Eighth Florida Infantry regiments. At Wilderness General Perry was seriously wounded and his Florida units were virtually wiped out.[33]

On May 16, as the Battle of Spotsylvania raged, the Confederate War Department ordered Finegan north to Virginia with his garrison troops to replace Perry and his demolished brigade. At that time the state of Florida was defended by six battalions, four infantry and two cavalry, each of about three hundred effectives, mostly middle-aged men and boys. Leaving the Fourth Florida Infantry Battalion behind in the Sunshine State, along with the First and Second Florida Cavalry battalions, Finegan traveled north with the three Florida infantry battalions that he had with him at Ocean Pond—the First, Second, and Sixth. Some of the Floridians, none of whom had ever served outside of their own state, deserted before they got to Virginia. Together with other small units of reinforcements from all over the south, Finegan's troops arrived in Petersburg, Virginia, south of Richmond on May 26. Second Lieutenant Luther Rice Mills of the Twenty-Sixth Virginia Infantry regiment observed a strange assortment of soldiers on the train. "Even Old Barney Finegan from the land of gophers and pine smoke has brought his little battalions along."[34]

Two days later at Atlee's Station, nine miles north of Richmond, Finegan's three battalions were reinforced by the remnant of Perry's three regiments, down to about two hundred officers and men. The Irishman consolidated Perry's veterans into a single unit, giving the new Florida brigade four infantry battalions for a total of about eleven hundred effectives, the only brigade in the army not to have at least one regiment. In fact Finegan's entire command was not much larger than one full regiment. Marching to the front, Finegan's Florida brigade joined the Army of Northern Virginia on May 29 near a crossroads inn called Cold Harbor. Lee assigned Finegan to the division of Irish-American Brigadier General William Mahone of Lieutenant General Ambrose Powell Hill's Third Corps. Mahone's division, posted at the left (north) end of the three-mile Confederate line, near the Totopotomoy River, had four original brigades, one each from the states of Alabama, Georgia, Mississippi, and Virginia.[35]

Finegan and his men received an immediate baptism of fire when light skirmishing broke out along the opposing entrenchments. The Floridians were in for more marching when Lee decided to move three of his divisions down to lengthen the right (south) end of his line near the Chickahominy River. The divisions were commanded by Mahone, Major General Cadmus M. Wilcox (also of Hill's corps), and Major General John C. Breckinridge, the former vice president of the United States. On the afternoon of June 2 the two brigades of Breckinridge's independent division from the Shenandoah Valley drove Federal pickets off Turkey Hill, a ridge that had been the scene of the Gaines Mill battle of two years earlier. Lee posted Wilcox's four brigades south of the ridge, to the extreme right of his line, with Breckinridge's two brigades to the immediate left of Wilcox in front of Turkey Hill. Mahone's five brigades, including Finegan's, were left in reserve behind the six brigades of Breckinridge and Wilcox, the only second line unit anywhere along Lee's front.[36]

Finegan's Florida brigade was deployed behind Breckinridge's right brigade of Brigadier General John Echols, temporarily commanded by Colonel George S. Patton, a Virginian from what was to become one of America's most prominent military families. Patton's brigade consisted of four infantry units—the Twenty-Second Virginia regiment (Patton's own command), the Twenty-Third and Twenty-Sixth Virginia battalions (formerly designated as regiments), and the Second Maryland Battalion, Breckinridge's reserve unit. (There was only one Maryland regiment in all of Confederate service. At first designated as the First Maryland regiment, it was later called the Maryland Line regiment to be deployed in two parts. The First Battalion was the cavalry half; the Second Battalion was the infantry half.)[37]

To the rear in support of Patton's three frontline Virginia units from left to right (north to south) were Lieutenant Colonel J. Parrar Crane's Second Maryland Battalion, Colonel David Lang's Second/Fifth/Eighth Florida Consolidated Battalion, and Lieutenant Colonel John M. Martin's Sixth Florida Battalion. General Finegan's headquarters was in the camp of his Sixth Battalion. Facing the three divisions of Generals Wilcox, Breckinridge, and Mahone across the line were the three divisions of Major General Winfield Scott Hancock's Second Corps, the predominantly Irish elite troops of Major General George Gordon Meade's Army of the Potomac.[38]

Grant instructed Meade to launch a massive three-corps assault against Lee's entrenched position between the Totopotomoy on the north and the Chickahominy on the south to begin at sunrise on June 3. On that day the Federals would penetrate the three-mile Confederate line at only one point of one small sector. The lone break came through Patton's brigade directly in front of the only position where the Southerners had any reserve strength. The gap was created when Lieutenant Colonel George Edgar allowed the picket line detachment from this Twenty-Sixth Virginia Battalion to move back out of the rain to the shelter of the main works. Patton's rifle pits were formed out of a salient at the base of Turkey Hill. At the center of this position was a battery of four guns, supported by two companies of the Twenty-Second Virginia regiment. Virginia infantrymen from the Twenty-Sixth and Twenty-Third battalions held down the rifle pits on opposite slopes that jetted out at an angle to the left and right of the artillery, like an inverted letter U.[39]

Union batteries all along the Cold Harbor front coordinated to open fire at 4:30 A.M. Ten minutes later Colonel L. O. Morris' Seventh New York Heavy Artillery regiment (serving as infantry) of Colonel John R. Brooke's Fourth Brigade of Brigadier General Francis C. Barlow's First Division of Hancock's Second Corps came swarming through Colonel Patton's vacated first line of Edgar's battalion and attacked the surprised Virginia gunners on Patton's main line. The Seventh New York was a huge regiment of sixteen hundred raw re-

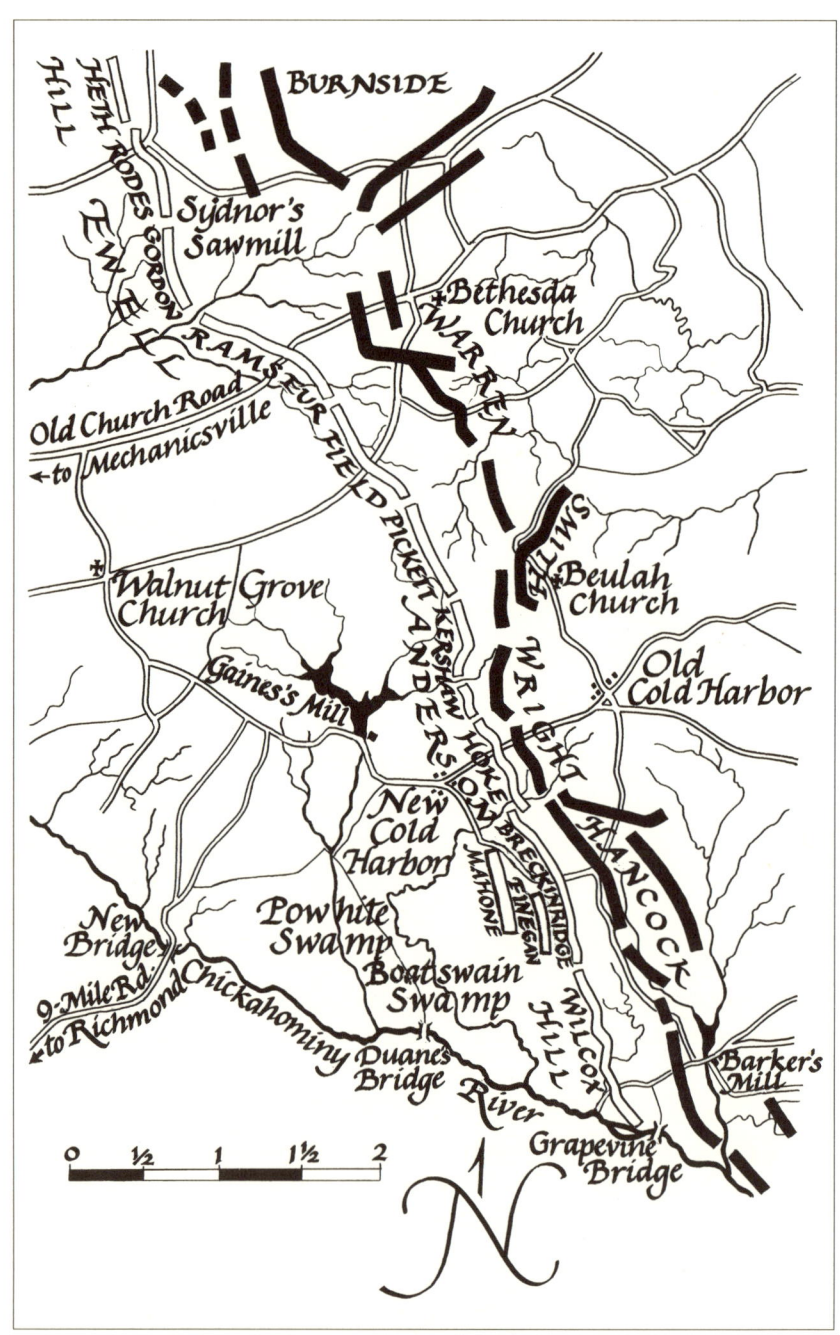

THE BATTLE OF COLD HARBOR, VIRGINIA
FRIDAY, JUNE 3, 1864 — 5:30 A.M. POSITIONS

cruits, mostly Irishmen. They were backed up on a second line by Colonel James A. Beaver's One-Hundred-Forty-Eighth Pennsylvania Infantry regiment, also of Brooke's brigade, also mostly Irishmen. Led by Brooke, the Federals captured the Confederate battery and turned the guns against Patton's Virginians on both sides of the inverted U. This Union success was, however, extremely brief.[40]

When the action opened on the Turkey Hill sector of the Cold Harbor battlefield, J. P. Crane's Maryland battalion was posted a mere fifty yards to the north rear (Patton's left, Brooke's right) of the heavily contested position, with David Lang's consolidated Florida battalion some seventy-five yards to the south rear. At 4:55 Crane's Marylanders reinforced the Virginians of the Twenty-Sixth Battalion on the north side of the inverted U, recaptured the battery and pushed Morris' right flank companies of the Seventh New York out of the main works. During Crane's counter-assault, Brooke was wounded and Beaver was killed. (Colonel O. H. Morris of the Sixty-Sixth New York took command of the brigade.) As a result the Irish Pennsylvanians were unable to move up quickly enough to support the Irish New Yorkers. At almost the same time that Crane took the initiative against L. O. Morris and the right flank companies of the New York regiment, Lang came up behind the south end of the inverted U, reinforced the Twenty-Third Virginia Battalion, and assaulted the left flank companies of the Irish New Yorkers, commanded by Major Joseph M. Murphy.[41]

General Finegan responded as aggressively as Colonels Crane and Lang. Private H. M. Hammill of the Sixth Florida Battalion described his commanding general's earliest reactions to the events of that morning:

> *Early in the morning of June 3—a misty, chilly morning—I had begun to boil my coffee and make for a rude breakfast, the men asleep about me. Suddenly the ragged crack of musketry began at the top of the slope, followed in a moment by the boom of cannon and the screaming of shells. A minute more the brigade was on foot, musket in hand, and General Finegan, on horse, was racing up and down the line, crying: "Get ready men; fall into line and charge!"*[42]

After sending the message for his two second line Florida battalions—the First and Second—to move up, Finegan personally led Colonel Martin's Sixth Battalion forward to reinforce Colonel Lang's consolidated battalion, already engaged with Major Murphy's companies of the Seventh New York. Arriving on the battlefield at 5:05 the Confederate Irishman, with enemy lead swirling around him, formed his two front-line Florida battalions into an assault wedge. Flushed with excitement and "slightly wounded," Finegan waved his hat and shouted exhortations as the men of Patton, Edgar, Lang, and Martin pushed the last two companies of Murphy's flank down the south end of the slope and out of the fight. The Second Florida Battalion came up to support the Twenty-Sixth Virginia Battalion and the Second Maryland Battalion on the Confederate left. The First Florida Battalion came up to support the Twenty-Third Virginia Battalion, the Second/Fifth/Eighth Florida Consolidated Battalion, and the Sixth Florida Battalion on the Confederate right.[43]

After forty minutes of hand-to-hand combat, the engagement at Turkey Hill between a single large Federal regiment of about sixteen hundred men and seven small Confederate battalions totalling about two thousand men ended at 5:20 with the Southerners again in control of the ridge. By that time General Grant's assault had already been smashed all along General Lee's front with staggering Federal casualties that may have gone as high as seven thousand. Cold Harbor was an overwhelming Confederate victory, with General Finegan having had the distinction of filling the only gap in the three-mile line. As the only general officer in that small sector, the Irishman commanded the Virginia, Maryland, and Florida troops between the divisions of Breckinridge on the left and Wilcox on the right, with the division of Mahone directly to the rear. Unfortunately, Old Barney proceeded to make three sizable mistakes on that same June 3, washing out his early morning success.[44]

The engagement at the south end of the Cold Harbor front at Turkey Hill represented the first time that Finegan had ever set foot on an active battlefield. Because of his lack of military experience, he failed to deploy troops on George Patton's original picket line, making the same error that George Edgar had made earlier. As a result, the retreating Irish New Yorkers of Murphy's last two left-wing companies filed into the abandoned works and immediately began digging in a mere fifty or sixty yards in front of the main Confederate breastworks. Between 5:30 and 7:30 A.M. native Hibernians Finegan and Murphy exchanged heavy musketry fire. At 8 the Florida Irishman shifted the Second Maryland Battalion and Patton's two Virginia battalions to the left with the rest of Breckinridge's troops and brought the First and Second Florida Battalions up to the main line, which meant that Finegan's own four Sunshine State units exclusively occupied the entrenchments behind the inverted U.[45]

From Patton's former picket line O. H. Morris reinforced Murphy with L. O. Morris. The Irishmen of the Seventh New York Heavy Artillery entrenched and poured canister and musketry into the Confederate works. Because of Finegan's first mistake, the Floridians had to keep their heads tucked down inside their own rifle pits. Captain James F. Tucker, commanding D Company of the Sixth Florida Battalion, described the situation:

> *The works we occupied were at the foot of a ridge and formed sort of an angle like an inverted U . . . we were exposed to enemy fire to such an extent that no one could either leave or approach our part of the line. All day orders from and reports to brigade headquarters had to be transmitted by word of mouth, or through the medium of a cap box passed from hand to hand, and ammunition was replenished in the same way.*

Having never before been exposed to such a bombardment, Finegan lost his composure and made his second mistake. At 9:30 A.M. he ordered a skirmish line assault. At 10 Major Pickens Bird and a small detachment, consisting of every fifth man of the Sixth Florida Battalion, charged the position held by the Irishmen of Joseph Murphy's companies. The mission was suicidal. Bird was seriously wounded and most of his men went down, killed or wounded. The others were forced to crawl back to their own works under heavy fire.[46]

The Irish general waited until dark to make his third mistake of

June 3—another skirmish line assault! While the men of the Sixth Florida Battalion continued to lick their wounds on the south side of the inverted U, Captain C. Seton Fleming, the son of Irish immigrants, and a small detachment of men from the Second/Fifth/Eighth Florida Consolidated Battalion were ordered by Finegan to advance from the north end. At 9 P.M. the youthful Fleming charged the position held by the Irishmen of L. O. Morris' companies. The men of the consolidated battalion suffered the same fate as the men of the Sixth. Fleming was killed and most of his men fell before they got anywhere near the enemy line. Ironically L. O. Morris survived that day but was killed the next day by a sharpshooter. Murphy then took command of the Seventh New York Heavy Artillery regiment. Finegan was praised by the Confederate high command for his early morning heroics, his subsequent blunders seemingly forgotten.[47]

Two days after the Battle of Cold Harbor, General Mahone brought up his Georgia brigade to relieve his Florida brigade in the trenches. Finegan's Floridians were resting in reserve on June 8 when they were reinforced by the men of the Fourth Florida Battalion and by the men of four independent companies of infantry who had been called up from Florida, leaving the Sunshine State with only two battalions of cavalry and no infantry. For the sake of appearances the Confederate War Department turned Finegan's five battalions and four companies into four infantry regiments. The ten companies of the Second/Fifth/Eighth Florida Consolidated battalion, in size the equivalent of a single full company, became the ten companies of the Second/Fifth/Eighth Florida Consolidated regiment under Colonel David Lang. The seven companies of the Sixth Florida Battalion, along with three of the independent companies, formed the Ninth Florida Regiment under Colonel John M. Martin. The six companies of the First Florida Battalion and four of the companies of the Second Florida Battalion formed the Tenth Florida regiment under Colonel Charles F. Hopkins. The seven companies of the Fourth Florida Battalion, along with the other two companies of the Second Battalion and the fourth and last independent company, formed the Eleventh Florida regiment under Colonel Theodore Brevard. With some of the wounded officers and men returning to active duty, Finegan's brigade was increased in numerical strength to about thirteen hundred effectives.[48]

At the same time that General Finegan was being reinforced, both Generals Lee and Grant were shifting their armies. On June 12 events in the Shenandoah Valley caused Lee to send the three divisions of Lieutenant General Jubal A. Early's Second Corps and General Breckinridge's division north to relieve that sector of the eastern theatre of operations. On that same day Grant, dissatisfied with his own sliding movements against Richmond, began marching five of his corps (II, V, VI, IX, XVI) over pontoon bridges south of the James River with the intent of striking the Confederate capital from south to north instead of from north to southeast. The Union commander's objective was the critical railroad town of Petersburg below Richmond, which linked and supplied the capital. General P. G. T. Beauregard, however, saved the Confederacy when he blocked the vanguard of Grant's army group out of Petersburg with elements of only two divisions of his detached corps. When Lee finally realized where Grant had gone, he rushed his remaining two corps (including Finegan's brigade of Mahone's division of Powell Hill's Third Corps) south to reinforce Beauregard's meager forces in front of Petersburg. The last and longest campaign of the War Between the States had begun—the Siege of Petersburg.[49]

Joseph Finegan's Floridians participated in the first two infantry engagements of the campaign: at Gurney's Farm on June 23, 1864, and at Stony Creek Depot on June 29–30. Finegan's trenches were near the Jerusalem Plank Road about a mile and a half south of Petersburg. On June 22 Grant tried to overextend Lee's supply lines by cutting the Petersburg and Weldon Railroad which linked central Virginia to northern North Carolina. When the two Union corps of Generals Hancock and Horatio Wright advanced, Lee countered with the three divisions of Hill's corps. But before the Federals could tear up much of the track, the Alabama, Georgia, and Virginia brigades of Mahone's division drove Hancock's men away from the Weldon Railroad and back to their entrenchments.[50]

Early the next morning Wright's Vermont brigade, commanded by Brigadier General Lewis Grant, began destroying another section of the track. Mahone used the four regiments of his Mississippi brigade, commanded by Brigadier General Nathaniel Harris, to chase the forward companies of the Vermont unit away from the railroad. When Harris' Mississippians pursued two of Lewis Grant's regiments, heavy fighting developed around Doctor Gurney's family farmhouse. Unfortunately for the Northerners, other units of Wright's VI Corps failed to come up in support of the Vermont brigade's front line. In the afternoon Mahone instructed Finegan to reinforce Harris. The Irishman aggressively poured his four regiments into the fray and by evening the eight Confederate regiments had overwhelmed the two Union regiments as 373 officers and men from the Fourth and Eleventh Vermont surrendered to Finegan. The men of the Florida brigade protected the railroad, while awaiting further instructions.[51]

On June 28 at 8 P.M. Mahone detached Brigadier General John C. C. Sanders' Alabama brigade and Finegan's Florida brigade from his division and marched the nine regiments south all night along the railroad line to Reams Station, nine miles below Petersburg. The night march was Mahone's response to Lee's orders to send an infantry detachment down to assist the cavalry divisions of Major Generals Wade Hampton and Fitz Lee (R. E . Lee's nephew), who were defending the Weldon Railroad against two divisions of Brigadier General James A. Wilson's detached Union cavalry corps. During the early morning hours of June 29, Mahone deployed his weary troops along the railroad from Reams Station on the north to Stony Creek Depot, two miles below Reams Station, on the south.[52]

At 7 A.M. Wilson advanced to the railroad at Reams Station, where he was unpleasantly surprised to find entrenched enemy infantry instead of Federal support infantry. Wilson rode south with a battalion of horse artillery and struck Mahone's infantry near Stony Creek Depot. Finegan rode up and down the line exhorting his Floridians to hold steady in spite of the enemy barrage. While Wilson's gunners and dismounted skirmishers were being distracted by Mahone's infantrymen, the main body of the two Confederate cavalry divisions smashed into the main body of the two Union cavalry divisions, taking about a thousand prisoners. During the remainder of June 29–30 various units of Federal troopers skirmished here and there with Confederate pickets, but were repulsed by troops commanded by Sanders and Finegan. All of this June 22–30 action south of Petersburg is remembered as the First Battle of the Weldon Railroad. Generals Grant, Meade, Hancock, Wright, and Wilson had failed to cut General Lee's supply line. General Finegan had capably led his brigade during the two important Southern victories at Gurney's Farm and Stony Creek Depot.[53]

Finegan and his men remained in their trenches just south of Petersburg for another month before becoming eyewitnesses to one of the most bizarre battles in American history. Beginning on July 25 the coal miners of the Forty-Eighth Pennsylvania Infantry regiment dug out a tunnel under the Confederate earthworks that was about 580 feet long and about 5 feet deep. On July 30 Federal engineers exploded an 8,000-pound black powder bomb in the shaft at 4:45 A.M., creating a hole in the ground that was 170 feet long, 60 to 80 feet wide, 30 feet deep. Two hundred and seventy-eight men of the Nineteenth and Twenty-Second South Carolina regiments were instantly killed or wounded, some of whom were blown 100 feet into the air. Thus began the infamous Battle of the Crater, sometimes referred to as the Petersburg Mine Assault.[54]

The three divisions of Major General Ambrose Burnside's IX Corps were coordinated to attack after the explosion. Burnside's men were so stunned by the scene in front of them, however, that they advanced into and through the crater very slowly, allowing Lee time to counterattack with his closest division—Mahone's. Finegan's brigade, on the extreme left of the division, was the nearest to the crater and as such was kept in the trenches in the case of a Union breakthrough. Harris' Mississippi brigade, to the right of Finegan, thinned out further to the right in order to cover the possibility of a Confederate withdrawal. Mahone charged with his three largest brigades, led by his own former brigade of Virginians under Colonel David A. Weisiger and, in spite of being heavily outnumbered, routed Burnside's confused troops. During the desperate fighting in the crater, Finegan ordered a continuous fire of musketry from his picket line. Private George Dorman of the Tenth Florida reported the Irishman's losses that day to be "only five to ten wounded." General Lee was so pleased by the successful counterattack that he made the on-the-spot decision to promote Mahone to major general and Weisiger to brigadier. General Grant best summed up the strange battle: "Our effort was a stupendous failure."[55]

Subsequent medical reports indicated that the Battle of the Crater was even more horrific than it first seemed. When the Union assault became bogged down in the huge hole, frustration and panic became commonplace. Some white Federal soldiers shot some black Federal soldiers in the back in a desperate attempt to break up the logjam. When Burnside fell back, enraged Confederates shot captured blacks in cold blood. Because the entrenchments of the Florida brigade were the nearest to the battlefield, Union prisoners, including blacks, were turned over to Finegan's command. Most whites were treated indifferently, while most blacks were treated poorly. There are several explanations for this. It was late in the conflict and the bitterness was intense on both sides. In point of fact, most of the Southerners and many of the Northerners considered the bombing to be an act of murder, not war. Also, there were so many wounded Confederates in a confined area that it became most difficult for the victors to effectively care for the even more numerous enemy wounded. Again, just as at Ocean Pond, there is no evidence to suggest that Finegan ordered the mistreatment of black prisoners. Likewise he did nothing to prevent it from occurring. The abuse of captured black troops at Ocean Pond and the Crater cannot be dismissed as a coincidence. The majority of Confederate commanding officers who were given charge of black prisoners did not leave a trail of ugly incidents behind them.[56]

By the middle of August the three corps of the Army of Northern Virginia were all on separate assignments. General Early was with the Second Corps in the Shenandoah; General Lee, in the absence of the severely wounded Lieutenant General James Longstreet, was with the First Corps north of the James River; and Generals Beauregard and Powell Hill were with the reinforced Third Corps south of the James. (Elements of Beauregard's independent corps had joined up with Hill's corps, which included Finegan's brigade of Mahone's division.) General Grant figured that the time was right to make another attempt at cutting off enemy supply lines into Petersburg by breaking up the Weldon Railroad. The resulting operations were known as the Battles of Globe Tavern and Second Reams Station or, taken together, the Second Battle of the Weldon Railroad. The first battle of June 23–30 had taken place south of Petersburg, just south of Reams Station. The first phase of the second battle, August 18–21, took place south of Petersburg but north of Reams Station near the Globe Tavern Inn.[57]

On August 15 Grant moved Major General Governeur K. Warren's Fifth Corps out of the trenches, while moving Burnside's Ninth Corps into Warren's vacated position. On August 18–19 elements of Warren's corps defeated elements of Hill's corps, captured the railroad line near Globe Tavern, and began to tear up the track. On August 20 Beauregard and Hill approved a plan of counter-assault proposed by Mahone, a Virginian who was familiar with that area. Early on the morning of August 21 nine Confederate brigades and a part of a tenth, all under "Little Billie" Mahone himself, advanced past the Poplar Spring Church along the Vaughn Wagon Road toward the Federal position on the Weldon Railroad. Unfortunately for the Southerners, the Northerners had spent the previous day entrenching.[58]

Mahone's idea was to attack with six brigades on a front line supported by three brigades on a second line; but because of faulty scouting reports there was a constant shifting of troop movements during the day. The right front of Mahone's moving wedge consisted of three brigades led by the five South Carolina regiments of Brigadier General Johnson Hagood's brigade of Major General Robert F. Hoke's all-Carolina division of Beauregard's Petersburg Corps. The left front of Mahone's moving wedge consisted of Finegan's Florida brigade on the extreme left, with Sander's Alabama brigade to the right of Finegan, and with Harris' Mississippi brigade behind Finegan. Harris was on sick leave and Sanders was killed by a sharpshooter during the march, leaving Finegan as the only general officer of the three brigades on Mahone's left front.[59]

At 10 A.M. the Floridians opened the attack on Mahone's left, spearheaded by Colonel Lang's consolidated Florida regiment and by Colonel Brevard's Eleventh Florida regiment. Strictly by bad luck

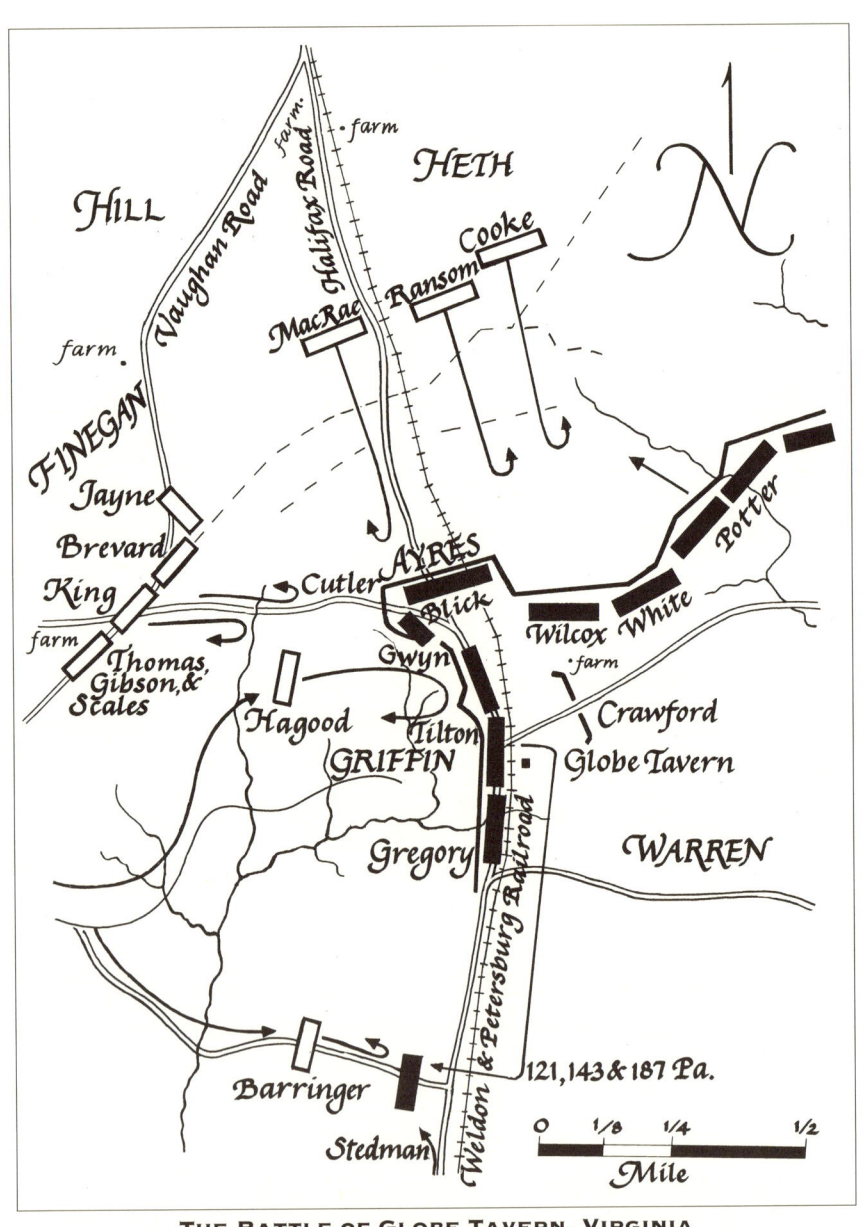

THE BATTLE OF GLOBE TAVERN, VIRGINIA
SUNDAY, AUGUST 21, 1864 — 10 A.M. POSITIONS

Finegan's men came up to about a hundred yards in front of the Federal breastworks of Brigadier General Edward Bragg's Iron Brigade (First Brigade, Fourth Division, Fifth Corps), a superb unit of Westerners from Indiana, Wisconsin, and Michigan. General Finegan, mounted to the rear of the Florida brigade and to the front of the Mississippi brigade, kept sending more companies of Floridians and Mississippians to Lang's forward position, but the Florida/Alabama front line was torn to pieces by the musketry and canister of the Sixth Wisconsin and Twenty-Fourth Michigan. When elements of all thirteen regiments in Finegan's left front sector began to break and run to the rear in panic, the Irishman rode forward and momentarily re-established his line with the able assistance of Lang, Brevard, Colonel J. Horace King of Alabama, and Colonel Joseph M. Jayne of Mississippi. When the Iron Brigade's position was reinforced by the Fourth and Seventh U.S. Maryland regiments of the Second Division of Warren's corps, Finegan's three brigades fell back in confusion, suffering heavy losses. The assault of General Mahone's nine brigades against nine brigades of General Warren failed all up and down the line. General Lee had lost the Weldon Railroad. General Finegan had lost much of his brigade.[60]

Globe Tavern casualties for the Florida brigade was better than one hundred men. In the next few months over four hundred of the Floridians were listed as absent because of sickness and about another two hundred deserted. By October of 1864 only some six hundred officers and men of the brigade were on the active roster, many of whom were mere teenagers. Mahone's division participated in the battle of First Hatcher's Run during this period, but Finegan's small band was kept in the trenches south of Petersburg in reserve. In December Powell Hill led a supply raid against Federal wagon camps in southern Virginia. Finegan's command was engaged in light skirmishing on the tenth of that month. The Irishman, like most Floridians, hated the cold of the Virginia countryside. With inadequate rations and clothing for his troops, he complained bitterly to Third Corps headquarters. The dispatches between General Hill (a Virginia West Point professional) and General Finegan were both amusing and ridiculous. Hill, with considerable patience, agreed with Finegan about the sad conditions in camp, noting correctly that there was absolutely nothing he could do about the situation.[61]

During that excessively cold winter of 1864–1865 Lee the army commander, Hill the corps commander, Mahone the division commander, and Finegan the brigade commander all took turns on sick leave. The four generals were never on the active list together on any single day in December or January. After a lull of about seven weeks U. S. Grant renewed the siege of Petersburg in early February of 1865. Powell Hill had just returned from sick leave. William Mahone was on sick leave. Joseph Finegan—homesick, depressed, and nearly frozen— wanted to go back on sick leave. This was not possible, however. As senior ranking brigade commander, the Irishman had the responsibility of leading Mahone's division.[62]

On February 5, 1865, six Union divisions south of Petersburg were ordered to move through Reams Station to Dinwiddie Courthouse and interrupt Confederate wagon trains believed to be using the Boydton Plank Road up into Petersburg. Brigadier General David M. Gregg commanded the two brigades of the Second Division of Irish-American Major General Philip H. Sheridan's Cavalry Corps; Warren commanded the three infantry divisions of his Fifth Corps; and Major General Andrew A. Humphreys commanded two of the infantry divisions of Hancock's Second Corps. The job of the lone cavalry division was to wreak havoc on the enemy supply wagons. The job of the five infantry divisions was to secure the area and protect the cavalry. The Federals occupied a two-mile line along a stream called Hatcher's Run near the Vaughn Wagon Road crossing, the scene of the First Battle of Hatcher's Run the previous October.[63]

Three Confederate infantry divisions held defensive positions in that same wooded area opposite the main Union line at Dabney's Saw Mill. These forces consisted of Major General Henry Heth's division of Hill's Third Corps and two divisions of the Second Corps under Major General John B. Gordon. Lee, concerned about the menacing enemy troop buildup south of Petersburg, ordered Finegan to take all five brigades of Mahone's division out of the trenches in support of Gordon. Late in the afternoon Colonel Robert McAllister's brigade of Humphreys' corps and Brigadier General John R. Cook's brigade of

Hill's corps became heavily engaged, but the winter sky turned dark before the fighting became general. Finegan's division was not engaged. Humphreys' two divisions were moved out of the Dabney's Saw Mill sector and replaced by the First Division of Wright's Sixth Corps, which was held in reserve.[64]

In the early morning hours of February 6, Gregg's cavalry division and one of Warren's infantry divisions were moved out to another sector of the battle known as Second Hatcher's Run, leaving three Northern brigades facing four small Southern brigades at Dabney's Saw Mill. Assured that he could hold his line, Lee instructed Finegan to march his five brigades north and back to their trenches. After three hours of slow, disorganized marching the Irishman received another dispatch from Lee. Finegan was to turn his men around and march them back south to the saw mill. It was 2 P.M. Fighting had broken out an hour earlier at Dabney's. Grumbling about the weather in particular and mumbling about army life in general, Old Barney did what he was ordered. Generals Lee and Hill were overseeing the fighting in other sectors of that Virginia battlefield. General Mahone was down sick. General Gordon was defending with an undersized command. General Warren could punch a hole in the Petersburg defenses and the fall of Richmond would follow. February 6, 1865, would prove to be the most glorious day in the life of General Finegan.[65]

An hour before Finegan had received the message to return, Warren had ordered Brigadier General Samuel W. Crawford of his Third Division to move elements of his three brigades out onto the Vaughn Wagon Road. Just east of the mill Brigadier General Henry Baxter's six regiments of the Second Brigade of Crawford's Third Division of Warren's V Corps collided with the five Virginia regiments of Colonel John S. Hoffman's brigade of Brigadier General John Pegram's division of Gordon's Second Corps. Both sides called for reinforcements. Unfortunately for Gordon, Pegram's other two brigades and all four of the brigades of Major General Bryan Grimes' division of the Second Corps were off on other assignments, so Gordon attacked Baxter with the three brigades of Brigadier General Clement A. Evans' division, while Crawford countered with the main body of his other two brigades.[66]

Baxter reformed Crawford's line at 2:45 and, with the Sixteenth Maine and Ninety-Seventh New York regiments leading the way, captured the abandoned mill, which some of Baxter's men had mistaken for a Confederate fort. Instead of a fortification that could be defended, the Northerners found "only a huge heap of saw dust." Evans advanced with his three brigades, spearheaded by the six Georgia regiments of Colonel John H. Baker's brigade. The four Confederate brigades of Gordon's corps pushed the three Union brigades of Crawford's division away from the ruins—but only for a few minutes. At 3:30 Warren reinforced Crawford with two of the brigades of Brigadier General Romeyn B. Ayres' Second Division of the V Corps. These ten fresh regiments of Marylanders, Delawares, and Pennsylvanians charged Gordon's weary Virginians, Georgians, and Louisianians and retook the demolished mill.[67]

Very late in this action the youthful Pegram was killed and Hoffman was seriously wounded. With no reserve troops left in the area, Gordon and Evans could only defend against Crawford and Ayres. For the purpose of clearing the Southerners off the Vaughn Wagon Road, General Meade instructed the three brigades of Brigadier General Frank Wheaton's First Division of Wright's VI Corps to leave their trenches in support of Warren's five brigades of Crawford and Ayres at Dabney's Saw Mill. As Wheaton moved out at 4:30 the five brigades of Finegan's division reached the battlefield. While the Federals were entrenching around the woods to the rear of the sawdust pile, Finegan conferred with Gordon and received permission to launch a two-wave frontal assault from west to east against the enemy position.[68]

The Irishman deployed four of his brigades in a double line with ten regiments on each line. The left (north) of the front line consisted of the five Alabama regiments of Colonel William H. Forney's (Sanders') brigade; to the right (south) of Forney, nearest to the mill, were the five Virginia regiments of Weisiger's brigade. The left of the second line, behind Forney, consisted of the six Georgia regiments of Brigadier General G. Moxley Sorrel's brigade; to the right of Sorrel, behind Weisiger, were the four Mississippi regiments of Harris' brigade. The four Florida regiments, under Lang, were held in reserve.

General Finegan rode to the front of General Weisiger's troops at five o'clock and ordered his front line forward. The Virginia soldiers found inspiration from the Florida general. One of them remembered the Irishman "in command on horseback with a citizen coat, Beaver hat, and walking stick." As the Virginians surged ahead, Finegan waved his hat and shouted: "On ye go brave lads; on ye go; on ye go."[69]

Finegan's two first wave brigades, led by the Eighth Alabama on the left and the Sixth and Sixteenth Virginia on the right, reformed with the remaining units of Gordon's four brigades and smashed into the Union line to the east of the mill, forcing Warren's troops out of their rifle pits. One of Colonel Forney's Alabamans recalled it well: "We drove them back easily and did it handsomely, nothing easier." Ayres' men resisted at first, but Crawford's men—hungry, tired, and discouraged—broke almost immediately, running into the woods in confusion. For the third time on that bloody day Confederate infantrymen filed into the trenches that protected a worthless mound of sawdust. At 5:20 Brigadier General Ranald MacKenzie's Second Brigade of Wheaton's First Division of Wright's Sixth Corps arrived to reinforce Warren's retreating Fifth Corps.[70]

The Florida Irishman, utilizing the excellent sense of timing that he had already demonstrated at Ocean Pond and Gurney's Farm, rode forward with General Harris' Mississippi brigade to the front of the mill and sent his second line of ten Georgia and Mississippi regiments into the fight just as MacKenzie's lead regiment, the One-Hundred-Twenty-First New York, took the field. Old Barney's second frontal wave, coming so soon after the first, intensified panic in Federal ranks as the New Yorkers of the One-Hundred-Twenty-First "threw down their muskets and ran back," while their officers unsuccessfully tried to turn them to the front with cries of "go back, go back!" General Sorrel recalled the moment of glory in his memoirs: "On February 6, my Georgians were hotly engaged in the afternoon and made a handsome, successful charge, which dislodged and forced back the Federals." General Finegan held Dabney's Saw Mill, but only momentarily.[71]

By six o'clock General Wheaton had steadied the ragged Union line with elements of the other fifteen regiments of his division, some of which were full size units. Just as it seemed likely that the Northerners would retake the mill again, Finegan came galloping up on his right (south) flank from west to east with the four small regiments of his own Florida brigade, waving his beaver hat and yelling encouragements to his troops. A Richmond newspaper reporter, who was with Weisiger's brigade, noted that Finegan's improvised third wave, in support of the Virginians and Mississippians on the Confederate right, staggered the Union left again. At that point in the battle the eight brigades of Crawford, Ayres, and Wheaton could not dislodge the nine brigades of Gordon, Evans, and Finegan. Within a few minutes, however, three more Union brigades came up in line of battle from the north and from the east. These troops were the thirteen regiments of the First Division of Warren's V Corps under Brigadier General Charles Griffin. At 6:30 the fresh divisions of Wheaton and Griffin, reinforcing the beleaguered divisions of Crawford and Ayres (total of eleven brigades), took the contested rifle pits for the third and last time.[72]

The Confederates, without a single soldier left in reserve, retired in good order west of Dabney's where they re-entrenched. Between 6:30 and 7 Finegan rode up and down the line, observing his formations, determining his next move. When he received scouting reports that Humphreys' Second Corps and Gregg's cavalry division were also in the area, he wisely held his position. The bloody battle for a useless piece of real estate had lasted six hours, with both sides taking possession of the mill three times. In the end Union numerical strength had won out. Finegan's efforts in the final hour and half had, however, helped to delay the Federal raid against Lee's wagon trains for twenty-four hours. It was an outstanding performance by the Irishman, his best and last of the war. At ten the next morning Meade ordered Crawford to drive the Southerners further away from Hatcher's Run and the Vaughn Wagon Road. A heavy rain came down all day long and several Federal probes were unable to penetrate the Confederate line. Crawford's men spent most of the day burying their dead.[73]

The February 5–7, 1865, Second Battle of Hatcher's Run was over. Grant had whittled down the rebellion one more time without much strategic gain. In three days of fighting, elements of three

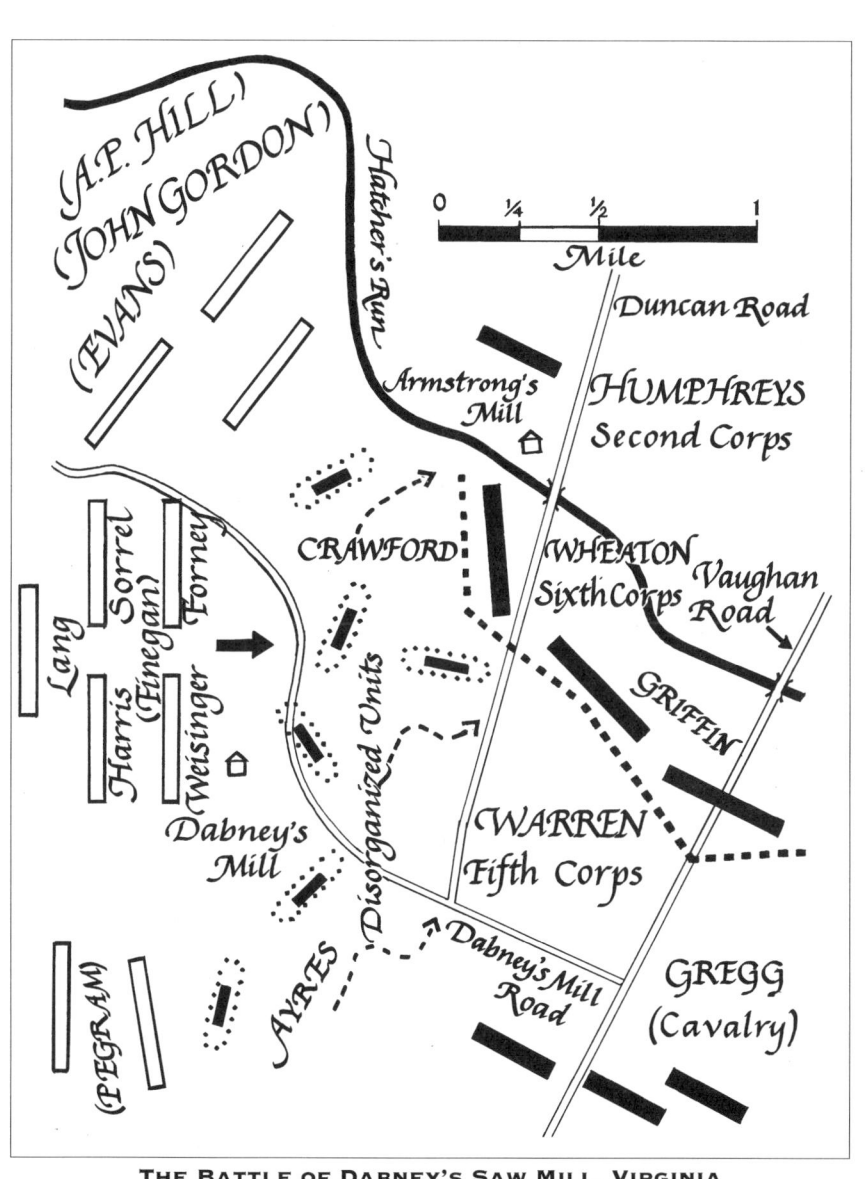

THE BATTLE OF DABNEY'S SAW MILL, VIRGINIA
MONDAY, FEBRUARY 6, 1865 — 5 P.M. POSITIONS

Union corps had been engaged for a total of 34, 517 effectives, of which 1,512 were killed, wounded, or missing. Confederate losses were about 1,000 out of the 13,835 officers and men engaged. Late on the second day Finegan had commanded all of the Southerners on the field, successfully holding off four enemy divisions with two divisions. Ironically many of the ranking Confederate officers and most of the members of the Richmond War Department never even knew that the Irishman commanded Mahone's division that day. General Cadmus Wilcox observed some of the action at Dabney's Saw Mill from high ground and recorded the events in his own personally written "battle-field notebook." Wilcox commended "Mahone's" tactics. Days later, when informed that the Floridian had been in field command, Wilcox took out his notebook, crossed out Mahone's name, and inserted Finegan's name above the crossings.[74]

Old Barney himself apparently did not realize how close the end was. If the Irishman had stuck it out until the conclusion of the great drama, his place in Confederate history would have certainly been higher than it was. When Mahone returned to active duty in March, Finegan requested transfer back to his former District of East Florida, claiming that the Sunshine State needed his "protection" from another possible Federal invasion. Aided by the influence of his friend, David Yulee, Finegan received his transfer from the War Department on March 20, 1865, leaving the tiny remnant of the Florida brigade behind in Virginia under Colonels David Lang and Theodore Brevard. A number of fellow officers never forgave the Irishman. Nineteen days after Finegan's transfer came through, Lee surrendered to Grant. During the summer of 1865 Finegan helped Secretary of War John C. Breckinridge to escape from Federal authorities through Florida to Cuba.[75]

The former Confederate general served a single term in the Florida State Senate (1865–1866) before moving to Savannah, where he served as a cotton broker, regaining some of his lost wealth. Having made enough money to purchase a home, Joseph and Rebecca returned to Florida and settled in the town of Rutledge, near Jacksonville, where he practiced law. Rebecca died on August 1, 1870, at the age of fifty-eight. Nine months later, J. Rutledge Finegan, the general's son, died tragically of yellow fever a few weeks prior to his thirty-third birthday. Poisoned forever by the bitterness of war, the older Irishman remained a "totally unreconstructed" Southerner to the end, hating everything Northern. Joseph Finegan died on October 29, 1885, at the age of seventy. He is buried in the Old City Cemetery in Jacksonville, his name misspelled on his own tombstone, appropriately symbolizing his obscurity! Many years after the conflict, when the descendants of Confederate Floridians realized that it had been General Colquitt and not General Finegan who had been in field command at Ocean Pond, a memorial honoring the unpopular Irishman was taken down. Unfortunately no marker has ever been erected along Hatcher's Run, south of Petersburg, Virginia, near the spot of an old saw mill, where General Finegan fought four Union divisions to a standstill in what was one of the very last offensive movements of the Army of Northern Virginia.[76]

NOTES

1. William C. Davis, ed. *The Confederate General* (Washington, D.C., 1992), vol. 2, p. 126; Dena Snodgrass, "General Joseph Finegan," a paper prepared for the Daughters of the Confederacy. Jacksonville: Museum of Southern History, 1951; Ezra J. Warner, *Generals in Gray* (Baton Rouge, 1983), p. 88.

Author's Note: The other four Irish brigadier generals were William M. Browne of Georgia, James Hagan of Alabama, Walter P. Lane of Texas, and Patrick T. Moore of Virginia.

2. Susan E. Burdett, "The Military Career of Brigadier General Joseph Finegan of Florida," Masters Thesis, Butler Library, Columbia University, 1930, p.1; Rose Shepard, "Florida Division Unveils Marker on Olustee Battlefield, Honoring General J. E. Finegan," *The United Daughters of the Confederacy Magazine* (July 1951), p. 19. (Author's Note: Joseph Finegan had neither a middle initial E. nor a middle name.)

3. George C. Bittle, "Florida Prepares for War, 1860–1861," *Florida Historical Quarterly (FHQ)* (October 1972), vol. 51, pp. 143–152; Laura A David, "Brigadier General J. Finegan," a paper prepared for the Daughters of the Confederacy. Jacksonville: Museum of Southern History, 1951; *New York Herald* Morning Edition, January 17, 1861; David L Yulee, Letter to Finegan, January 10, 1861, the Yulee collection, Civil War Papers, 1861–1865. Gainesville: P. K. Yonge Library of Florida History, University of Florida.

4. Dorothy Dodd, "The Secession Movement in Florida," *FHQ* (October 1933), vol. 12, pp. 10–11, p. 65; John E. Johns, *Florida During the Civil War* (Gainesville, 1963), p. 38; William H. Nulty, *Confederate Florida: The Road To Olustee* (Tuscaloosa, 1990), pp. 15–16; Official Records of the Armies (ORA), vol. 14, p. 494.

5. Mark M. Boatner, III, ed. *The Civil War Dictionary* (New York, 1959), p. 279, p. 286; Burdett, p. 5; Patricia L. Faust, ed. *Historical Times Illustrated: Encyclopedia of the Civil War* (New York, 1986), p. 259, p. 264.

6. Allen W. Jones, "Military Events In Florida During the Civil War, 1861–1865," *FHQ* (July 1960), vol. 39, p. 42; National Archives, Washington D.C., "Report of the Naval Planning Committee to Gideon Welles,

July 5, 1861"; ORA, vol. 6, pp. 398–399, vol. 7, pp. 573–578; Official Records of the Navies (ORN), vol. 12, pp. 261–319; Alice Strickland, "Blockade Runners," *FHQ* (October 1957), vol. 36, p. 88.

7. Florida State Archives, Tallahassee, Compiled Military Service Records of General and Staff Officers from the State of Florida, series 989, reel No. 1; John Milton, Letterbook Typescript, 1861–1863. Tampa: Florida Historical Society Library, University of South Florida; ORA, vol. 6, p. 430; Yulee War Papers, 1861–1865, Report of General James Trapier to Governor John Milton, January 20, 1862. Yonge Library, University of Florida.

8. William W. Davis, *The Civil War and Reconstruction in Florida* (Gainesville, 1913), p. 50; J. J. Dickinson, *Confederate Military History: Florida* (Atlanta, 1899), vol. 16, pp. 49–52; *Florida Sentinel*, June 17, 1862; Don Hillhouse, *Heavy Artillery and Light Infantry . . .* (Jacksonville, 1992), pp. 17–21; ORA, vol. 6, p. 309.

9. Edwin C. Bearss, "Military Operations on the St. John's River, Florida, September–October, 1862," *FHQ* (January 1964), vol. 42, pp. 232–233; Burdett, pp. 7–8; Frederick T. Davis, "Engagements at St. John's Bluff, St. John's River, Florida, September–October, 1862," *FHQ* (October 1936), vol. 15, pp. 77–78; ORA, vol. 14, pp. 120–121, pp. 128–132; ORN, vol. 13, pp. 324–325.

10. Thomas W. Higginson, "Up the St. John's," *Atlantic Monthly* (September 1865), vol. 16, pp. 311–313; Ellen E. Hodges, and Stephen Kerber, "Children of Honor: Letters of Winston and Octavia Stephens, 1861–1862," *FHQ* (July 1977), vol. 56, p. 46; Ellen E. Hodges, and Stephen Kerber, "Rogues and Black Hearted Scamps: Letters of Winston and Octavia Stephens, 1862–1863," *FHQ* (July 1978), vol. 57, pp. 66–68; ORA, vol. 14, pp. 133–137.

11. Bearss, p. 81; Howell Cobb, District of Middle Florida Dispatches, November, 1862 to September, 1863, Charles P. Cooper to Cobb, December 5, 1862. Athens: Hargrett Rare Book and Manuscript Library, University of Georgia; Finegan letter to Yulee, January 16, 1863, Civil War Papers, 1861–1865; *Florida Sentinel*, October 6, 1862; Hillhouse, p. 42; ORA, vol. 14, p. 139; ORN, vol. 13, p. 357; Margaret Anderson Uhler, ed. "Civil War Letters of Major General James Patton Anderson," *FHQ* (October 1977), vol. 56, p. 152.

12. Daniel Ammen, *The Atlantic Coast* (New York, 1883), pp. 70–71;

Columbus, Oh., *Daily Sun*, October 6, 1862; Hillhouse, p. 44; Johns, p. 73; Nulty, p. 56; ORN, vol. 13, p. 356; William J. Schellings, "Blockade Duty on the Florida Coast: Excerpts from a Union Navy Officer's Diary," *Tequesta* magazine (1955), vol. 15, pp. 55–72; Jerome Tourtellotte, *A History of K Company of the Seventh Connecticut . . .* (Hartford, 1910), pp. 47–48.

13. Dickinson, p. 55; Hillhouse, p. 47; ORA, vol. 14, p. 665; Mamie Morris Webster, "Brigadier General Joseph Finegan," a paper prepared for the Daughters of the Confederacy, August 12, 1940. Jacksonville, Museum of Southern History.

14. Charles Cooper to Howell Cobb, December 5, 1862. Dispatches. National Archives, Washington D.C., Confederate General Joseph Finegan and Staff Officers, Record Group No. 109, Microcopy M331, Roll 93.

15. Finegan letter to Yulee, January 30, 1863, Civil War Papers, 1861–1865; Thomas W. Higginson, *Army Life in a Black Regiment* (Williamson, Mass, 1971), p. 98; ORA, vol. 14, p. 838; Edward C.Williamson, ed. "Francis P. Fleming in the War for Southern Independence: Soldiering with the Second Florida Regiment," *FHQ* (July 1949), vol. 28, p. 46.

16. D. Appleton, ed. *The American Annual Encyclopedia* (New York, 1863) vol. 3, p. 413; Caroline M. Brevard, *A History of Florida . . .* (Deland, Florida: State Historical Society, 1925), vol. 2, p. 85; Burdett, p. 13; ORA, vol. 11, p. 610.

17. George H. Dorman, *Fifty Years Ago: Reminiscences of 1861–1865* (Jacksonville, 1912), p. 34; Higginson, *Army Life*, p. 106; Hillhouse, pp. 53–55; ORA, vol. 14, pp. 226–227, p. 234.

18 Dickinson, p. 54; *Florida Times Union*, "Diary of Dr. Alfred Walton," October 30, 1893; Webster Merritt, *A Century of Medicine in Jacksonville and Duval County* (Gainesville, 1949), p. 56; ORA, vol. 14, p. 228; Samuel Proctor, "Jacksonville During the Civil War," FHQ (April 1963), vol. 41, p. 352.

19. D. H. Donald, *Inside Lincoln's Cabinet: The Civil War Diaries of Salmon P. Chase* (New York, 1954), p. 190; Orvid L. Futch, "Salmon P. Chase and Civil War Politics in Florida," *FHQ* (January 1954), vol. 32, pp. 163–188.

Author's Note: Grant's army group consisted of the Army of the Potomac, the Army of the James, and the Army of the Shenandoah, while

Sherman's army group consisted of the Army of the Cumberland, the Army of the Tennessee and the Army of the Ohio.

20. Robert L. Clark, "Northern Plans for the Economic Invasion of Florida, 1862–1865," *FHQ* (January 1950), vol. 28, pp. 262–270; ORA, vol. 28, part 2, p. 129, vol. 35, part 1, pp. 278–279; George Winston Smith, "Carpetbag Imperialism in Florida, 1862–1868," *FHQ* (October 1948), vol. 27, pp. 99–104.

21. George Baltzell, "The Battle of Olustee (Ocean Pond) Florida," *FHQ* (April 1931), vol. 9, pp. 207–208; David James Coles, "A Fight, a Licking, and a Footrace: The 1864 Florida Campaign and the Battle of Olustee," Tallahassee: Masters Thesis, Florida State University, 1985, pp. 35–36; ORA, vol. 35, part 1, p. 280; Michael P. Watson, "Sunshine State Saved," *America's Civil War* (March 1990), pp. 44–45.

22. Samuel Jones, "The Battle of Olustee or Ocean Pond, Florida." *Battles and Leaders of the Civil War (BL)*, (New York, 1883), vol. 4, p. 77; Cornelius Murphy, "The Battle of Olustee," Prepared for the Civil War Centennial Commission, Library of Congress, 1964, p. 6.

23. Mark F. Boyd, "The Federal Campaign of 1864 in East Florida," *FHQ* (July 1950), vol. 29, p. 10; Burdett, pp. 17–21; Joseph R. Hawley, "Comments on General Jones' Paper," *BL*, vol. 4, p. 79; *New York Herald*, February 20, 1864; *The New York Times*, February 20, 1864; Nulty, pp. 82–101; ORA, vol. 35, part 1, p. 282, pp. 594–595.

24. Baltzell, pp. 208–210; Boyd, pp. 13–16; Coles, pp. 75–79; Johns, p. 197; Nulty, p. 124; ORA, vol. 35, part 1, pp. 296–298; Gideon Welles, Diary, Library of Congress, vol. 10, p. 535.

25. James J. Dancy, "Reminiscences of the Civil War," *FHQ* (July 1958), vol. 37, pp. 74–75; Hillhouse, p. 66; Johns, p. 196; Murphy, p. 9; Nulty, p. 122; ORA, vol. 35, part 1, p. 331; Watson, p. 47.

26. Luis F. Emilio, *History of the 54th Massachusetts* (New York, 1968), pp. 151–152; Hawley, pp. 79–80; Richard A. Martin and Daniel L. Schaper, *Jacksonville's Ordeal By Fire: A Civil War History* (Jacksonville, 1984), pp. 180–182.

27. Vaughn D. Bornet, "A Connecticut Yankee Fights at Olustee," *FHQ* (April 1949), vol. 27, pp. 251–253; Benjamin W. Crowninshield, *First Massachusetts Cavalry . . .* (Boston, 1891), pp. 259–260; Henry Little, *Seventh New Hampshire . . .* (Concord, 1896), pp. 210–211.

28. Boyd, pp. 25–26; James H. Clark, *The 115th New York . . .* (Albany 1865), pp. 73–74; Emilio, p. 162; Hawley, p. 80; ORA, vol. 35, part 1, p. 305; Abraham J. Palmer, *The History of the 48th New York . . .* (Brooklyn: Veterans Assoc.), 1885, p. 133.

29. *New York Tribune*, March 1, 1864; Julien C. Yonge, ed. "The Occupation of Jacksonville, February 1864, and the Battle of Olustee: Letters of Lt. C. M. Duren, 54th Massachusetts Regiment U.S.A.," *FHQ* (January 1954), vol. 32, p. 282.

30. Baltzell, pp. 220–221; *Jacksonville Peninsular*, April 7, 1864; Grady McWhiney, and Perry D. Jamieson, *Attack and Die: Civil War Military Tactics and the Southern Heritage* (Tuscaloosa, 1982), p. 11; Nulty, p. 203.

31. Dorman, p. 5; *The Floridian and Journal* (Tallahassee), March 21, 1864; Hillhouse, pp. 72–74; Gary L. Loderhose, *A History of the Ninth Florida Regiment* (Richmond, 1988), pp. 54–55; Nulty, pp. 170–188; ORA, vol. 35, part 1, p. 332.

32. *Atlanta Intelligencer*, March 2, 1864; Coles, pp. 139–165; John McElroy, *Andersonville: A Story of Rebel Military Prisons* (Toledo, 1879), p. 163; Richard McMurry, "The Battle of Olustee," *Civil War Times Illustrated* (*CWTI*) (January 1978), vol. 16, pp. 19–20; ORA, vol. 35, part 1, pp. 329–330; *Savannah Morning News*, March 3, 1864.

33. *Charleston Daily Courier*, February 24, 1864; Loderhose, p. 56; Murphy, pp. 14–15; ORA, vol. 35, part 1, p. 338.

34. George D. Harmon, ed., "Letters of Luther Rice Mills—A Confederate Soldier," *North Carolina Historical Review* (July 1927), vol. 4, p. 299; ORA, vol. 35, part 2, p. 485, p. 488, p. 491.

35. Jed Hotchkiss, *Confederate Military History: Virginia* (Atlanta 1899), vol. 3, p. 467; James I. Robertson, *General A. P. Hill: The Story of a Confederate Warrior* (New York, 1987), p. 278.

36. Douglas Southall Freeman, *Lee's Lieutenants: A Study In Command* (New York, 1944), vol. 4, p. 508; Hillhouse, pp. 78–79; Loderhose, p. 70; ORA, vol. 36, part 3, pp. 833–836.

37. *Charleston Mercury*, June 8, 1864; Clifford Dowdey, *Lee's Last Campaign: The Story of Lee and His Men Against Grant*, 1864 (Boston, 1960), p. 297; W. W. Goldsborough, *The Maryland Line in the Confederate Army* (New York, 1972), p. 126; Hillhouse, p. 80; ORA, vol. 36, part 1, p. 369.
Author's Note: Lee, Hill, Mahone, Echols, and Patton were all Virgin-

ians. Colonel George S. Patton was the grandfather of the famous World War II general of the same name.

38. Dickinson, p. 158; Dorman, pp. 6–8; Goldsborough, p. 127; Zack C. Waters, "Tell Them I Died Like a Confederate Soldier: Finegan's Florida Brigade at Cold Harbor," *FHQ* (October 1990), vol. 69, p. 166.

39. Louis J. Baltz III, *The Battle of Cold Harbor: May 27–June 13, 1864* (Lynchburg, Va., 1994), p. 137, p. 139; Burdett, p. 15; Dowdey, p. 297; Goldsborough, p. 127; Hillhouse, p. 80; James H. Lane, "History of Lane's North Carolina Brigade," *Southern Historical Society Papers* (*SHSP*), vol. 9, p. 244; ORA, vol. 36, page 2, p. 103; Larry Wakefield, "Charge Most Regretted," *Military History* magazine, (June 1986), p. 29.

40. Bruce Catton, *A Stillness at Appomattox* (New York, 1953), p. 182; *The New York Times*, June 7, 1864; Glen Tucker, *Hancock the Superb* (Dayton, 1980), p. 224; Waters, pp. 170–171; Jeffry Wert, "One Great Regret," *CWTI* (February 1979), pp. 33–34.

41. Baltz, p. 140; Gregory Jaynes, *The Killing Ground: Wilderness to Cold Harbor* (Alexandria, Va., 1986), pp. 158–160; Martin T. McMahon, "Cold Harbor" BL, vol. 4, p. 217; Noah Andre Trudeau, *The Wilderness to Cold Harbor: May–June 1864* (Boston, 1989), pp. 284–289.

42. H. M. Hamill, "A Boy's First Battle," *Confederate Veteran* magazine (CV), vol. 12, p. 540.

43. Francis P. Fleming, *Florida Troops in Virginia* (Jacksonville, 1884), p. 99; *Philadelphia Weekly Times*, June 5, 1864; Fred L. Robertson, *Soldiers of Florida* (Tallahassee, 1903), p. 329.

44. Shelby Foote, *The Civil War: A Narrative, Red River to Appomattox* (New York, 1974), p. 291; Freeman, *Lee's Lieutenants*, vol. 4, p. 508; Gary W. Gallagher, ed., *Fighting for the Confederacy: The Personal Recollections of General Edward Porter Alexander* (Chapel Hill, 1989), p. 409.

45. Finegan letter to Yulee, June 8, 1864, Civil War Papers, 1861–1865; Andrew A. Humphreys, *The Virginia Campaign of 1864 and 1865* (New York, 1883), p. 183; Loderhose, pp. 75–76; Waters, p. 172.

46. Hamill, p. 541; Hillhouse, p. 81; James F. Tucker, "Some Florida Heroes," *CV*, vol. 11, p. 363.

47. Dickinson, pp. 158–159; Loderhose, pp. 77–78; McMahon, p. 217; ORA, vol. 35, part 1, pp. 349–350; James Tucker, p. 364; Waters, pp. 174–176.

48. Dorman, p. 5; Bertram H. Groaens, ed. "Civil War Letters of Colonel David Lang," *FHQ* (January 1976), vol. 54, p. 363; Hillhouse, p. 83; ORA, vol. 35, part 1, pp. 333–335; *Richmond Daily Dispatch*, June 12, 1864.

49. William S. McFeeley, *Grant: A Biography* (New York, 1981), p. 173; Horace Porter, *Campaigning With Grant* (New York 1897), p. 224; T. Harry Williams, *P. G. T. Beauregard: Napoleon In Gray* (Baton Rouge, 1955), p. 235.

50. Joseph P. Cullen, "The Siege of Petersburg," *CWTI* (August 1970), vol. 9, no. 5, p. 15; Freeman, *Lee's Lieutenants*, vol. 3, pp. 453–454; Gordon W. McCabe, "Defense of Petersburg," *SHSP*, vol. 2, p. 274.

51. G. G. Benedict, *Vermont in the Civil War* (Burlington, Vt 1886), vol. 1, pp. 475–479; Maurice S. Fortin, ed. "Colonel Hilary A. Herbert's History of the 8th Alabama . . ." *Alabama Historical Quarterly* (1977), vol. 39, p. 144; A. Mulholland St. Clair, *The Story of the 116th Pennsylvania . . .* (Philadelphia, 1903), pp. 270–279; ORA, vol. 40, part 1, pp. 501–502.

52. Dorman, pp. 13–14; Herbert, p. 145; Hillhouse, p. 88; McCabe, p. 275; *Petersburg Express*, June 25, 1864; *Richmond Daily Dispatch*, June 27, 1864; James I. Robertson, *General Hill*, p. 287.

53. Michael A. Cavanaugh, *Sixth Virginia Infantry*, (Lynchburg, Va., 1988), p. 49; Freeman, *Lee's Lieutenants*, vol. 4, p. 540; Herbert, p. 145; Hillhouse, pp. 90–91; Humphreys, p. 229; ORA, vol. 40, part 1, pp. 627–642; *Richmond Whig*, July 2, 1864; Fred Robertson, *Soldiers of Florida*, p. 207.

54. Cullen, pp. 17–18; John W. Daniel, "Graphic Account of the Battle of the Crater," *SHSP*, vol. 33, p. 364; Benjamin H. Trask, *Sixteenth Virginia Infantry* (Lynchburg, Va., 1988), pp. 36–39.

55. Cavanaugh, pp. 49–50; Dorman, p. 11; Herbert, pp. 153–154, p. 156, p. 197; Hillhouse, pp. 99–101; Loderhose, pp. 127–129; Bell Irwin Wiley, ed., *General G. Moxley Sorrel's Recollections of a Confederate Staff Officer* (Wilmington, S.C., 1987), p. 258.

56. Finegan letter to Yulee, July 30, 1864, Civil War Papers, 1861–1865.

57. Frances H. Kennedy, ed., *The Civil War Battlefield Guide* (Boston, 1990), p. 253; E. B. Long, *The Civil War, Day By Day: An Almanac, 1861–1865* (New York, 1971), pp. 556–558.

58. Edwin C. Bearss, "Battle of the Weldon Railroad," Petersburg Na-

tional Park Document No. D23, pp. 1–21; John Horn, *The Petersburg Campaign: The Destruction of the Weldon Railroad* . . . (Lynchburg, Va., 1991), pp. 84–93; Charles H. Porter, "Operations Against the Weldon Railroad," Papers of the Military Historical Society of Massachusetts, vol. 5, p. 246.

59. Bearss Document No. D23, p. 64; Cavanaugh, p. 56; Freeman, *Lee's Lieutenants*, vol. 3, pp. 588–589; Herbert, p. 174; Horn, pp. 96–97; Loderhose, p. 133; Trask, p. 41.

60. O. B. Curtis, *History of the 24th Michigan* . . . (Detroit, 1891), p. 273; Dorman, p. 16; Freeman, R. E. Lee, vol. 3, p. 487; Johnson Hagood, *Memoirs of the War of Secession* (Columbia, S.C., 1909), p. 290; Nathaniel Harris, *Movements of the Confederate Army in Virginia* (Jackson, Miss., 1901), p. 34; Hillhouse, p. 104; Horn, pp. 98–99; ORA, vol. 42, part 1, p. 430, p. 484, pp. 541–542, part 2, pp. 1188–1189.

61. Dickinson, p. 159; Hillhouse, p. 111; National Archives, ANV Compiled Service Records: Florida, Microcopy M251; ORA, vol. 42, part 3, p. 613, p. 621, p. 774, vol. 46, part 2, pp. 1143–1149.

62. Finegan letter to Yulee, January 27, 1865, Civil War Papers, 1861–1865; Herbert, p. 176; National Archives, ANV Inspection Report, November 30, 1864.

63. Foote, vol. 3, pp. 784–785; Humphreys, pp. 312–314; Loderhose, p. 140; *The New York Times*, March 2, 1865; *Richmond Whig*, February 8, 1865.

64. Nelson M. Blake, *William Mahone of Virginia* (Richmond, 1936), p. 63; Noah Andre Trudeau, *The Last Citadel* . . . (Boston, 1991), pp. 312–317.

65. Hillhouse, p. 115; ORA, vol. 46, part 2, p. 1206; Trudeau, p. 318.

66. Hotchkiss, p. 527; James I. Robertson, p. 311; Trudeau, p. 318–319.

67. Catton, p. 383; Cullen, p. 27; Humphreys, p. 314; Trudeau, p. 319.

68. Dickinson, p. 160; Foote, vol. 3, p. 785; Trudeau, pp. 319–320.

69. Cavanaugh, p. 58; Harris, pp. 58–59; Herbert, p. 178; Trask, p. 46; as cited in Trudeau, p. 320.

70. Giles Buckner Cooke, Diary, 1864–1865 (Richmond), p. 14; Herbert, p. 178; Humphreys, p. 315.

71. Harris, p. 59; Sorrel, p. 272 as cited in Trudeau, p. 320.

72. Lang, pp. 364–366, p. 368; *Richmond Enquirer*, March 2, 1865;

William H. Rogers, *History of the 189th New York . . .* (New York, 1865), p. 202.

73. Hillhouse, p. 116; Loderhose, p. 141; Trudeau, p. 321.

74. Trudeau, p. 332; Cadmus M. Wilcox, "Notes on the Richmond Campaign, 1864–1865," Library of Congress, pp. 182–183.

75. A. J. Hanna, *Flight Into Oblivion* (Richmond, 1938), pp. 128–129; ORA, vol. 46, part 2, p. 1128, vol. 51, part 1, pp. 407–408.

76. W. C. Davis, p. 127; Old City Cemetery Records, Jacksonville; Shepard, p. 26; Warner, p. 88.

Father Rebel: Abram J. Ryan

Poet-Priest-Patriot-Philosopher

Of the Lost Cause

Father Abram J. Ryan

The Man and the Myth

IN VIEWING ANY PAST PERIOD OF TIME the bipartisan onlooker must make all observations through historical glasses. This is sometimes referred to as objectivity. The same onlooker must avoid making observations about past events, and subsequent judgments about them, through modern glasses. A lack of objectivity is sometimes referred to as political correctness. Glasses with nineteenth century lenses will produce a clear and consistent image of the man who came to be known as the Reverend Abram J. Ryan, a devout Catholic clergyman and an outspoken Yankee-hating unreconstructed Southern patriot. However, glasses with 1990s lenses will reflect the image of a man whose attitudes about race justify the modern scene of an angry group of Civil Rights era protesters marching around the Ryan Square in Mobile, Alabama, demanding that the monument to the white oppressor from the male-dominated Church be unceremoniously torn down. Ryan's philosophy of life fit perfectly within the places and times in which he lived. He is an enigma only if viewed through the wrong specs.

During the Know-Nothing movement of the 1850s there was more anti-Catholic activity in the North than in the South, for the simple reason that there were many more Catholic immigrants seeking jobs in the North than in the South. When the War Between the States broke out in 1861, more than one Catholic bishop felt compelled to remind President Abraham Lincoln that Catholic soldiers, many of whom were immigrant victims of native American bigotry, would fight to preserve the Union but not to free the slaves. At that time Abolitionism was the number one enemy of Catholicism in the United States. Abolitionists in general and New England Congregationalists in particular were vehemently anti-Catholic. These New

Englanders were, in fact, the ancestors of the folks who had perfected the witch hunt. Catholics took the opposite side of whatever side the abolitionists were on. There was not a single prominent American Catholic in the abolitionist movement.

Catholic bishops, clergy, and laity residing in the North, along with their Protestant neighbors, tended to support the Union cause without much said about slavery. Catholic bishops, clergy, and laity residing in the South, along with their Protestant neighbors, tended to support the Confederate cause without much said about slavery. Most white Americans—Protestants and Catholics, Northerners and Southerners—believed blacks to be inferior to whites. This was because of the way they were raised and was not necessarily a matter of personal racial hostility in the modern sense. There was absolutely nothing unusual about an 1861 Southern-born-and-bred Catholic priest supporting the Southern cause. In fact it was the natural thing for him to do.[1]

For Abram J. Ryan the conflict was a Holy War of Revolution, with Southerners defending their homeland against the godless Northern invaders. After the war Ryan, as the poet-priest of the South, became one of the true champions of an ideal, fostered on Southern Nationalism, known as the philosophy of the "Lost Cause." It was very simple. Southerners are a committed Christian people, so their cause was morally right and just. God was, in fact, on the side of the South. The Confederacy was, however, defeated. Therefore the righteous cause was betrayed from the outside by Lincoln and his black Republicans and from the inside by Southern political traitors and by disloyal army officers, such as Lieutenant General James Longstreet who was wrongly blamed for the disaster at Gettysburg. Ryan's works embodied the literary and poetic expression of the mixed sentimentality, religiosity, and patriotism that was the Lost Cause. The priest, a native Virginian, was an articulate spokesman for the original nineteenth-century Southern Evangelical Christian Right.[2]

Since Father Abram's post-bellum philosophy was considered something of an embarrassment to the modern Church, several twentieth-century Catholic historians covered the facts with fiction. The process of "updating" Ryan took place slowly over the years with the appearance of a few inaccurate articles. Finally in 1959 the historical

Ryan was replaced completely by the mythical Ryan. That was the year when Monsignor Harold J. Heagney's absurd book, *Chaplain In Gray: Abram Ryan,* was published in New York by P. J. Kenedy and Sons. It was a work of pure nonsense. Unfortunately thousands of copies were sold. Some Civil War bookstores still carry original printings. Not only did Heagney not know much about Ryan, he didn't know much about the War Between the States. The fictitious Ryan of Heagney, apparently with the ability to bilocate, defied Union General Benjamin Butler in New Orleans at the same time that he was conversing with the friendly, smiling Confederate General Stonewall Jackson in Virginia. The same fictitious Ryan was outgoing, soft-spoken, forgiving and loving toward all mankind. The historical Ryan never met Generals Butler or Jackson, and was never associated for even one minute with the Army of Northern Virginia. The historical Ryan was a very private person, brooding and melancholy, with a strong temperament.[3]

Over the course of the next thirteen years two other monsignors—Charles C. Boldrick of Kentucky and Oscar Hugh Lipscomb of Alabama—worked hard to set the record straight. Their articles, which appeared separately in July of 1972, were sometimes contradictory and almost entirely out of any sequence, but historical. Boldrick especially was researching in all of the right directions, while compiling a valuable set of reference materials. By 1980, however, a few confusing essays had also appeared in various small publications as the result of interest generated by Boldrick and Lipscomb. The only certain aspect of these latest efforts was their uncertainty. Sometimes the reader was left adrift with a need to fill in the blanks. "Father Abram Ryan was born in Cleonmell, Ireland, or Norfolk, Virginia, or Hagerstown, Maryland, or somewhere in Kentucky."[4] The works of Abram J. Ryan have, for the most part, been preserved. The man has been forgotten. This is unfortunate because the man was one of the most beloved heroes of the Old South. Twenty-first century historians, like Humpty-Dumpty, will have to put all of the Ryan pieces back together again. Some clues are provided here.

THE POET-PRIEST

MATTHEW ABRAHAM RYAN AND MARY COUGHLIN RYAN, natives of the town of Clonmell in County Tipperary, Ireland, emigrated to the United States in 1836 and settled in Norfolk, Virginia, with their daughter, Eleanor. Matthew was a pack-on-back peddler who sold his goods to Irish Baltimore and Ohio Railroad workmen along the Virginia-Maryland border. The family frequently wandered from town to town. A son, Matthew Abraham Ryan, Jr., was born at Norfolk on February 2, 1838, and was baptized in Hagerstown, Maryland, at St. Mary's Church on June 4, 1838. To avoid confusion with his father's name the parents called the boy Abraham. At confirmation the name Joseph was added, so that Matthew Abraham Ryan, Jr., became Abraham Joseph Ryan. Late in 1842 a younger brother, David, was born in Hagerstown. Matthew, Mary, Eleanor, Abraham, and David moved to St. Louis, Missouri, in 1848 where the family operated a general store.[5]

The three Ryan children were educated by the Christian Brothers. Idealistic Abraham, who was outstanding in prose, poetry, music, singing and public speaking, decided at the age of sixteen in 1854 to become a priest and missionary in the Vincentian Order. He attended the Vincentian school, "The Barrens," near St. Louis and was followed a few years later by David, who looked up to his older brother in every way. After graduating in 1858, Abraham finished his sacred studies at a college now known as Niagara University near Buffalo, New York, eventually to be followed again by David. The Vincentian community recalled the elder Ryan brother to St. Louis on July 4, 1860, and judged him to be ready for the priesthood ahead of schedule. At the age of twenty-two Abraham Joseph Ryan was ordained in St. Louis on September 12, 1860, by Bishop Peter Richard Kenrick. The enthusiastic young cleric wrote a poem about his own priesthood.

> To the higher shrine of love divine
> My lowly feet have trod.

I want no fame, no other name
Than this a priest of God.[6]

The early priestly years were a whirlwind of activities as Father Abraham, an outstanding preacher, was assigned to a "Mission Band" that traveled through the small towns of eastern Missouri and central Illinois. At St. Patrick's Church in La Salle, Illinois, Ryan's sermon about the virginity of Mary, Mother of God, was so moving and so well received that it drew attention in both the religious and secular press. During this same tour of duty the young priest divided his preaching time between sermons about the physical and spiritual purity of the Virgin and speeches about the political purity of Jefferson Davis and the Southern Confederacy. When Abraham Lincoln was sworn into office as President of the United States in March of 1861, he was dubbed "Father Abraham" by Missouri's slaves. In protest the pro-secession and pro-slavery Father Abraham Joseph Ryan forever shortened his name to Father Abram Joseph Ryan, signing all future documents as the Reverend Abram J. Ryan, the name for which he would become famous.[7]

Father Abram, a native Southerner who spoke and sang beautifully with a deep resonant drawl without the mix of an Irish brogue, saw no conflict between his devotion to God and country. However, his Vincentian superiors, who carefully maintained a neutral stance about the war in bitterly divided Missouri, became alarmed about the unwelcome partisanship and assigned their gifted young preacher as a theology professor at Niagara, with the belief that his new duties would distract him from wartime issues. They were wrong. Ryan proceeded to inform staff and students alike that the Union cause, especially abolitionism, was morally reprehensible. This did not play well in Buffalo. During the summer of 1862 a series of events began to unfold that would forever change the life of the pro-Confederate priest.[8]

On August 20 David Ryan, who was still following in his brother's steps, was sent back from Niagara to The Barrens by the same group of which Abram was a member. The two brothers, who were close, felt that this action was taken in retaliation for the elder Ryan's unpopular views. In point of fact, David was held back solely because he was not mature enough or intelligent enough to compete academically at Niagara. Instead of returning to The Barrens, however, the younger Ryan traveled to Marion County, Kentucky, where he intended to register at St. Mary's College for the fall semester. Plans were abruptly changed when a Confederate army recruiter arrived at the college on about the same day as David. As a patriotic Southerner with the same political views of his brother, David Ryan enlisted on September 10, 1862, at Springfield, Kentucky, in K Company of the Eighth Kentucky Cavalry of Colonel Roy S. Cluke, a regiment in the famed "Kentucky Cavalier" brigade of Brigadier General John Hunt Morgan. Nine days before David joined the Confederate cavalry, Abram was dismissed from the Vincentian Order. When given a direct order to discontinue his political crusade, he politely refused and separated himself from the Vincentian Fathers. But even without a congregation Father Abram was still a priest at a time when young preachers were much needed on the frontier.[9]

In January of 1863 Ryan accepted an invitation to return to St. Mary's Church in Peoria, Illinois, where he was fondly remembered for his preaching tour of 1860. On April 11 of that year Private David Ryan, age twenty, was killed in action at the Battle of Monticello, Kentucky. A shocked Father Abram finally received the bad news at Peoria on July 17, 1863. Not only was his beloved younger brother dead at the hands of the Yankees, but David's final resting place was also unknown. At the age of twenty-five Abram J. Ryan suffered a nervous collapse. He lost weight and got sick. His hair turned prematurely gray. In despair the future poet-priest of the South wrote "In Memory of My Brother," a poem filled with the foreboding and mystery that characterized his later works.

> *A grave in the woods with the grass o'ergrown,*
> *A grave in the heart of his mother*
> *His clay in the one lies lifeless and lone;*
> *There is not a name, there is not a stone,*
> *And only the voice of the wind maketh moan*
> *O'er the grave where never a flower is strewn*
> *But his memory lives in the other.*[10]

The marriage record for St. Mary's, Peoria, holds the signature of the Reverend Abram J. Ryan for the last time on October 4, 1863. With a terrible sadness and bitterness in his heart the priest made his way south on horseback to search for his brother's grave. The War Between the States was no longer a lecture hall debate. It was deeply personal. Although he may not have realized it at the time, Ryan had begun a mission that would last for the rest of his life. After wandering about Kentucky in vain for information about David, Father Abram met a young Irishman by the name of Miles Driscoll. Determined to join the Confederate Army of Tennessee, Ryan and Driscoll rode southeast, finding the army encamped at Chattanooga on November 21, 1863. A London newspaper correspondent took note. "Father Ryan arrived at camp. His orderly, Miles Driscoll, brought him to me." This brief statement has caused considerable confusion among historians. It was assumed that Ryan "de facto" became an army chaplain in spite of the fact that no chaplain named Father Abram J. Ryan was ever listed by the supposedly careless Richmond War Department. In reality Ryan never applied for a chaplain's commission. The day after he arrived the priest saw General Braxton Bragg at his headquarters atop Missionary Ridge, offering his services to the Confederate commander. On that same day of November 22 Bragg, who instinctively trusted few people, appointed Father Abram to his own personal staff as an aide-de-camp.[11]

Three days later, during the Battle of Missionary Ridge, Ryan performed the temporary duty of courier by relaying messages from Bragg to Major General John C. Breckinridge's regimental commanders along the crest of the ridge, a high-risk assignment to say the least. Included among the line officers was Irish-born Major John G. O'Neill, acting regimental commander of the Tenth Tennessee Infantry, an Irish-Catholic unit from Nashville. Later that same afternoon of November 25, Ryan and Driscoll got caught up in the fighting along with the Nashville Irishmen and the other soldiers of Brigadier General William B. Bate's division. During the Union charge up the hill, Miles Driscoll was killed while Abram Ryan continued to fire his musket until ordered to fall back across the crest with the Tenth and

Thirtieth Tennessee regiments. The fighting ground to a halt after 7 P.M. with the Federals in full possession of Missionary Ridge.[12]

Father Abram then joined the Confederate chaplains who ministered to the Southern wounded. According to one observer "in every fallen man he thought he saw his brother. At every unmasked mound he wondered if it held his brother." Ryan served General Bragg in various capacities until the spring of 1864 when the restless priest began wandering again in another futile attempt to locate David's grave. During this period a Confederate spy was arrested in Chicago who claimed to be "Father Ryan of Peoria." Federal authorities accepted the identity and banished the bogus priest to Canada. When word of this affair reached the real Ryan in Tennessee, he became even more bitter than ever about the Unionists, describing them as "lying abolitionist Huns." (In the eyes of Ryan and most other Southerners the "abolitionists" included Lincoln and all of his Republicans.) It was also at this time that the increasingly grim, humorless priest began to identify himself in his own personal writings as a religious revolutionary whose purpose in life was to preach the gospel of Southern Nationalism. His political leanings never in any way conflicted in his own mind with his duties as a clergyman. Most of these early writings of the wandering Ryan have been lost for better than a century.[13]

On April 2, 1865, the signature of the Reverend Abram J. Ryan appeared on the baptismal register of St. Joseph's Church in Knoxville, Tennessee. The following Sunday, April 9, was Palm Sunday. It was also the same day that General Robert E. Lee surrendered to General U. S. Grant. When Ryan received the bad news during Holy Week he went into church and wept just as hard as if he had lost another brother. Returning to the parish house in another state of despair he scribbled out a poem on the back of a used envelope. President Abraham Lincoln was assassinated a few days later on Good Friday, April 14. When news of the assassination reached Knoxville during Easter Week, the priest's depression was lifted. Entering the church again Father Abram J. Ryan knelt in prayer giving thanks to the Lord for the death of a man he referred to as an "arrogant abolitionist ape." Even years later Ryan branded the prairie politician as a "modern anti-

Christ." His views on Lincoln were shared by most of the Southern people who considered John Wilkes Booth to be a patriot.[14]

On May 24, 1865, the poem scribbled on the envelope during Holy Week, called "The Conquered Banner," was published in New York's *Freeman's Journal* with the author listed as a certain "Moina" who was, of course, Abram J. Ryan. The "Poet-Priest of the South" was born. The English critic Henry Houghton praised it as "the finest work to come out of the American Civil War." When Father Abram was interviewed about it a few months later he said, "I wrote it in little over an hour, and wrote it out of a broken heart."

"The Conquered Banner" literally rallied the Southern people around the flag during their darkest hour. The poem was soon carried by the major newspapers throughout the South.

> *Furl that Banner, for 'tis weary;*
> *Round its staff 'tis drooping dreary*
> *Furl it, fold it, it is best;*
> *For there's not a man to wave it,*
> *And there's not a sword to save it,*
> *And there's not one left to lave it*
> *In the blood which heroes gave it;*
> *And its foes now scorn and brave it*
> *Furl it, hide it, let it rest.*
> *For though conquered, they adore it;*
> *Love the cold, dead hands that bore it!*
> *Weep for those who fell before it!*
> *Pardon those who trailed and tore it!*
> *But, oh! wildly they deplore it,*
> *Now who furl and fold it so.*
> *Furl that Banner, softly, slowly!*
> *Treat it gently—it is holy—*
> *For it droops above the dead.*
> *Touch it not—unfold it never,*
> *Let it droop there, furled forever.*
> *For its people's hopes are dead!*[15]

Later the poet-priest himself explained the popularity and significance of "The Conquered Banner," which was, of course, the Confederate Battle Flag, the very symbol of the Old South.

I never had any idea that the poem would attain celebrity. No doubt the circumstances of its appearance lent it much of its fame. In expressing my own emotions at the time, I echoed the unuttered feelings of the Southern people, and so "The Conquered Banner" became the requiem of the Lost Cause.

This was an extremely accurate self-assessment. During the era of "Reconstruction" (1865–1876), when the Congressional Radical Republicans tried their best to humiliate and punish the people of the defeated South, the wandering priest did indeed become the poet-philosopher of the Southern Confederacy's Lost Cause. Another such Lost Cause poem was written by Ryan shortly after "The Conquered Banner," although it would not become well known until years later. Called "The Southland," this work contained all of the haunting sentiments that made Ryan's poetry so special.

Yes, give me the land where the ruins are spread.
And the living tread light on the hearts of the dead.
Yes, give me a land that is brest by the dust,
And bright with the deeds of the downtrodden just.
Yes, give me a land with a grave in each spot,
And names in the graves that shall not be forgot.
Yes, give me the land of the wreck and the tomb,
There is a grandeur in graves, there is glory in gloom.[16]

Eyewitness accounts and church records place Father Abram in three separate parishes of Irish-born Bishop Patrick Feehan's Tennessee Diocese between 1864 and 1866. Prior to his stay at Knoxville he assisted at St. Mary's Church (later Immaculate Conception) in Clarksville above Nashville near the Kentucky border, where he refused to visit wounded Federal soldiers, explaining that "Yankees need be attended to by Yankee doctors and clergy." Mr. and Mrs. John J. Conroy of Montgomery County and St. Mary's became lifelong friends of the poet-priest. Hannah Murray Conroy described the private Ryan: "While he was of a rather meditative mind, still he was a most entertaining person and a very pleasing conversationalist." After the priest had moved to Georgia in 1866 he sent a letter to the Conroys stating firmly his opinion of Reconstruction era Northern Republican Carpetbaggers. The sentiments expressed in the letter became a recurring theme of Ryan's, namely that the "abolitionist Huns" were at the gate which, in many respects, they were.

> *The country is completely deluged with Yankees—Yankee ministers–Yankee school masters and school marms–Yankee merchants—Yankee doctors and lawyers—and Yankees of every calling imaginable. They are pouring in—pouring in—everyday and heaven knows when they will stop. I suppose, however, it is the same all over the South. Every car from Virginia is crammed with them. They are as bad as the plague of locust in olden time. You see that my feelings about these people have undergone no change. I cannot bear them—'tis no use trying.*

Ryan even wrote a poem about the evils of Reconstruction, which he called "Destruction." "Lost! Lost! Lost! Not the sign of hope was nigh, in the sea, in the air, or in the sky."[17]

Following his stays at Clarksville and Knoxville he assisted at St. Mary's, Nashville. All three of these Tennessee assignments lasted but a few months each. This was part of the character of Ryan. Although he was generally well liked by the parishioners he served, the wandering continued along with the endless search for David's grave. In the summer of 1866 the poet-priest drifted down to Augusta in French-born Bishop Augustine Verot's Diocese of Georgia. A friend from the Augusta years wrote about Abram's priestly ministry over the next year and a half.

> *Father Ryan served as an assistant at St. Patrick's Church and attended the missions of Macon, a laborious work due to the*

difficulties of transportation. He was well received, as ever, by the families he served, and was always welcome in their homes. After the train journey to Macon, he would proceed to the Ward plantation, thirty miles distant, the only Catholic family in that county. He would offer Mass in their parlor, and would later relax himself by playing on their melodeon.[18]

The outstanding preaching and writing abilities of Father Abram caught the attention of Bishop Verot. The wandering priest was a rare gem in the American Church of the 1860s, an era in which the vast majority of U.S. Catholic clergymen were of foreign birth. Not only was Ryan native-born, but he was also Southern-born-and-bred. Best of all he was a Confederate veteran. During the war Verot had taken a neutral stance on the issues of secession and slavery, all the while supporting the Southern war effort. The Catholic bishop and his tiny flock were looked on with some suspicion by Georgia's huge Protestant majority. Augustine Verot was, however, an energetic and resourceful church leader. When the Georgia public school system was organized following the war, the Catholic bishop, with residence at Savannah, founded two of his own parish schools, one in Savannah, the other in Augusta. By 1868 plans were under way for a third school, in Macon. In order to finance his emerging parochial school system, Verot used the talents of Ryan by appointing the poet-priest first as founding editor of the short-lived *Pacificator* and then as founding editor of *The Banner of the South*, the Augusta-based official publication of the Catholic Church in Georgia.[19]

The purpose of the paper was to provide a true Southern identity for Georgia's Catholics and to raise funds for diocesan schools. Father Abram took to his task with great enthusiasm, demonstrating for the first time the enormous influence he held as a writer. The main features of the weekly newspaper were Ryan's own editorials and poems about Southern patriotism, plus heroic short stories about traditional Southern chivalry. The religious paper was, in fact, secular in its appeal. In his very first editorial Ryan boldly stated his philosophy of the Lost Cause.

Submission to might is not surrender to right. We yield to the one—
but shall never yield to the other . . . We shall do our best, therefore,
to save from oblivion the memories and traditions of the
Confederacy. Whoever in the South who is ashamed of these had
better not read The Banner of the South *. . . Amid the questions*
which agitate the present, we should never lose pride in our past.[20]

Within a few months the eight-page weekly had a circulation of
about six thousand readers, the majority of whom were Protestants.
Even more important, Ryan's fame spread when his rally-'round-the-
flag editorials and poems were reprinted in the *Southern Press.* Not
only did a number of non-Catholics donate to the Catholic schools
but surprisingly some of them actually enrolled their own children in
the schools as Ryan put it "in order to foster a better understanding of
our proud Southern heritage." (This represented one of the very first
times in American history when Christian private schools were attended for reasons other than religious education, beginning a long-
standing tradition that continues to this day.) By 1869 *The Banner of*
the South was promoting Bishop Verot's controversial plan to create a
public-financed private school for Negro children. (There were no
public schools for blacks at that time in Georgia.) Father Abram,
whose own personal racial theories were similar to those of the late
Senator John C. Calhoun, successfully raised money for the project. In
an April 1869 editorial he reminded his readers of the necessity "to
keep the races totally separate in all things, most especially education,"
all of which created the need for a special Negro school so that "the
most advanced of them acquire a few simple skills for the betterment
of Southern society." According to the poet-priest, however, if all else
failed, the sending of blacks to school would serve to "prevent them
from discovering mischief." Throughout this successful promotion
Father Abram consistently demonstrated a genuine warmth toward
the black children he described as "little ones of God."[21]

Also in 1869 the second of Ryan's two most famous Lost Cause
poems appeared in several editions of *The Banner of the South.* Even
more popular than "The Conquered Banner," "The Sword of Robert
E. Lee" gave the poet-priest universal fame throughout the South. At

the age of thirty-one Father Abram J. Ryan, a parish priest with the most simple of life-styles, had emerged as a true champion of the long-suffering Southern people.

> *Out of its scabbard! Never hand*
> *Waved sword from stain as free,*
> *Nor purer sword led braver band,*
> *Nor braver bled for a brighter land*
> *Nor brighter band had a cause so grand,*
> *Nor cause a chief like Lee!*
> *Forth from its scabbard all in vain*
> *Bright flashed the sword of Lee;*
> *'Tis shrouded now in its sheath again;*
> *It sleeps the sleep of our noble slain,*
> *Defeated, yet without a stain,*
> *Proudly, and peacefully.*[22]

In spite of his personal popularity and fund-raising success, Father Abram, who had a low threshold of tolerance for any negative criticism, lasted less than two years as a Georgia newspaper editor. In 1870 the opinionated priest got into a meaningless squabble with the temperamental bishop. Not surprisingly the disagreement was in regard to politics, not church doctrine. Responding in the paper to an off-the-wall question about "the Church of Rome's policies about dealing with the darkies," Ryan offered an equally off-the-wall published response: "The Holy Father is infallible in regards to spiritual matters, such as the virginity of Mary, but not as to the rights of the Southern people." The poet-priest was perfectly correct about separation of Church and State, but his strange answer didn't fit the strange question. He was, in fact, very clever at not directly answering troubling questions. Verot, trying to uphold his image in the American Church of being an enlightened Southern churchman, was annoyed by the publication of such crank letters in the diocesan newspaper and by Ryan's serious attempt to explain everything away by references to patriotism. Verot truly believed in the equality of all men; Ryan truly believed, as did nearly all white Americans of that period, in the equality of all white men. Some harsh words were exchanged by the two proud clergymen.[23]

One day Father Abram J. Ryan, fiercely independent as always, got on his horse and departed Georgia for Alabama. After he left, Bishop Verot sent a letter to Leopold T. Blume and Patrick Walsh, publishers of *The Banner of the South*. In an effort to clarify the dispute, the bishop praised the priest for his commitment to the Church but questioned "his excessive political views and involvement with the night riders." This quote, made in 1870, confirms the independent statement made many years later by historian Don C. Seitz in his book *The Dreadful Decade*, about the origins of the Knights of the Ku Klux Klan: "Some others who went in were sentimentalists. One was Father Abram J. Ryan, the poet-priest, who became Grand Chaplain of the Order." According to the testimony of Verot, Ryan joined the Klan in Augusta sometime between 1868 and 1870. According to the account of Seitz, Ryan became national Klan chaplain at Mobile sometime after 1870. Since the Ku Klux Klan was a secret organization, the duties of Grand Chaplain have not been recorded. How long Ryan remained within the organization is unknown.[24]

In July of 1870 the signature of the Reverend Abram J. Ryan appeared in the baptismal register at St. Patrick's Cathedral, Mobile, Alabama. Irish-born Bishop John Quinlan, who would become a close personal friend, invited the poet-priest to live with him in the cathedral parsonage. Like Verot, Ryan wrote to Blume and Walsh.

At last, after some wanderings and pleasant meetings and mournful goodbyes at Savannah, Atlanta, and Macon, I have reached Mobile. The Banner of the South *must never furl its folds.*

Bishop Verot and his publishers tried unsuccessfully to replace the poet-priest of the South with another editor. It was an impossible task. The newspaper of the Diocese of Georgia did, indeed, fold its furls in September 1870.[25]

A month later a great tragedy was experienced by the people of the Old Confederacy. General Robert E. Lee died. National mourning followed. The poet-priest was invited to participate in a Lee memorial at the town hall of Eufaula, Alabama, outside Mobile. The place was packed with people who had come from rural areas many miles away as well as from the surrounding towns. Several prominent citizens delivered long speeches which could not be understood by the gathered throng because of poor acoustics. When Father Abram rose with a remarkable sense of the dramatic, the hall fell silent. The poet-priest walked up and down the aisles slowly, reciting his own "Sword of Lee" with a magnificent, powerful voice that could be heard even by onlookers outside the building. It was a spellbinding performance. Ryan's recitation was so well received and caused such a commotion that he repeated it in many different locations over the coming years.[26]

During his seven-year stay with the bishop in the Mobile cathedral, Father Abram filled the church with his preaching while moderating a youth group called the "Children of Mary." Most of the poems and sermons of this period would eventually be published. A terrible outbreak of the deadly yellow fever struck the Alabama coast between 1870 and 1872. The poet-priest risked his own life by ministering to the thousands of sick, often accompanied by his friend, Rabbi Abraham Laser. (It should be noted that the Klan's Grand Chaplain served sick blacks as well as sick whites.) Rose, the rabbi's daughter, described the desperate situation:

> *Like Father Ryan, my father refused to leave the city to its fate, but had remained on during the dreadful pestilence and heat, working day and night among the stricken. In the midst of his labors, there was always by his side or close at hand the dauntless, tireless Catholic preist.*[27]

Ryan's health began to fail seriously and he never fully recovered. In order to recuperate he went on a European pilgrimage from November 1872 until April 1873. The highlight of this trip occurred in Rome when Father Abram presented Pope Pius IX, a kindred conservative spirit, with a collection of his own religious poems on Marian themes. Also during the St. Patrick's Cathedral period the poet-priest edited the New Orleans diocesan newspaper for the Irish-born Bishop J. D. Perce, all the while residing with Bishop Quinlan in Mobile.

This was the second coming of the Georgia Banner of the South, featuring even more patriotic poems and tales of Southern valor. With Reconstruction still in effect and with federal troops still camped in the South, the poet-priest continued to warn the Southern people that the Huns were still at the gate. By this time Ryan's editorials had become strict and even puritanical about most forms of human behavior. In one *Morning Star* editorial he detailed a "Dress Code for Women in Church," reminding Catholic ladies to have their heads covered, Mary-like, in the presence of the Blessed Sacrament. Oddly enough many Baptist ladies then began the practice of keeping their bonnets on in church, a practice that continues in some places to this very day. It would seem that some Louisiana subscribers took every word that the poet-priest wrote as the literal truth. The *Morning Star* also featured Ryan poems that could be sung, including "Sentinels of Song."

> *When falls the soldier brave,*
> *Dead at the feet of wrong.*
> *The poet sings and guards his grave,*
> *With Sentinels of Song.*

In 1877 Quinlan rewarded his dynamic friend with the pastorate of St. Mary's Church on the Old Shell Road at the very outskirts of the Mobile city limits. Ryan loved the country assignment but at the age of forty he again contracted yellow fever in 1878. By then the priest had written dozens of poems, some of which had appeared in newspapers from the Atlantic Ocean to the Mississippi River.[28]

While recovering from his latest illness, Father Abram was visited by his nearest neighbor on Old Shell, a lawyer named John Hannis Taylor. A mutual friend of the two men was John L. Ropier, editor of *The Register* (Mobile). Taylor and Ropier convinced the poet-priest to publish a selection of his works. The result was put together in book form at Mobile in 1879, titled *The Poems of Father Ryan: Patriotic, Religious, and Miscellaneous*. It was soon reprinted in Baltimore. (The fortieth and last edition of the national best-seller was published at New York in 1929 by P. J. Kenedy and Sons.) All proceeds were donated by Ryan to the widows and orphans of Confederate veterans.

The publication of his first book made Ryan a nationally known celebrity. In 1880 a reporter from *The New York Times* came all the way to Old Shell Road to interview the famed poet-priest of the South. Ryan took an immediate disliking to the Yankee and his questions. When he was asked how he knew for sure that he had been born in Virginia, the priest looked the reporter straight in the eye and retorted with a slow drawl: "My mother told me. She ought to know."[29]

The following year John Quinlan asked his friend and most famous cleric to take another parish assignment, but Father Abram politely declined because of his poor health. After eleven years in Mobile, the one place he identified as home, the poet-priest moved to the quiet Gulf resort town of Biloxi, Mississippi, where his sermons and more religious poems were published in 1882, many expressing a melancholy appropriate for a funeral. The title of the second book was *A Crown for Our Queen*. Some of the poems were dedicated to individuals. Some had no titles or references at all.

Jesus! bless thee!
Mary! love thee!
Angels! guide thee!
Till above thee
Beams the beauty of the throne
Gleams the glory of the crown.
And then Oh! then! look down
And pray for us to weep
That out of sorrows deep
We may in gladness rest
From earth unto the skies
And meet thee there
Where all is fair
Where sorrow ends, and sighs.[30]

Father Abram resided at St. Mary's Church near the Beauvoir plantation home of a kindred Southern spirit—former President Jefferson Davis. Varina Davis was charmed by the eloquent poet-priest. (Ryan could be extremely charming when he wanted to be and extremely non-charming when he did not want to be.) Davis, who also suffered from chronic illness, exchanged correspondence with the priest. The President's favorite poem from the Ryan collection, called "The March of the Deathless Dead," contained a classic mixture of Lost Cause sadness, sentimentality, and patriotism.

> *Gather the sacred dust*
> *Of the warriors tried and true,*
> *Who bore the flag of a Nation's trust*
> *And fell in a cause, though lost, still just,*
> *And died for me and you.*

The poet-priest's national fame grew tremendously in 1883 when he was invited by Lieutenant General Jubal A. Early to participate in dedication ceremonies for a statue of Lee at the general's tomb in Lexington, Virginia. The Second Corps commander and his Army of Northern Virginia veterans were in the process of canonizing Lee as the patron saint of the Lost Cause. Ryan, the native Virginian, had become the leading poet and one of the leading spokesmen of that movement. Just as he had done thirteen years before at Eufaula, the priest rose and solemnly recited his "Sword of Lee." Grown men wept; women fainted. Major General Daniel Harvey Hill, at that time the President of Arkansas University and one of the most insubordinate, obstinate, cynical, and arrogant members of the Confederate high command, rushed forward and held onto Ryan with both hands and would not let go. Father Abram's performance on that day passed into Southern folklore.[31]

A fellow poet, Charles W. Hubner, attended that dedication to General Lee and left behind a full description of the post-Reconstruction Ryan, age forty-five, at the height of his enormous influence.

> *He was of medium height, his shoulders, though somewhat stooping, were broad, and firmly set upon them was a remarkable massive head, with a very broad and full forehead. His dark hair, brushed back negligently, was long and curly, gracefully framing his pale face, a face whose expression was sad and somewhat austere;*

but it was filled with power, carved here and there, with lines and furrows which with mute eloquence indicated a strong, passionate nature, but subdued and held in check by a mighty inward purpose; the face exhibited the results of great spiritual struggles, of sorrow and of suffering. His voice was clear, his elocution simple, direct, emphatic. But the most expressive feature of that strong pathetic face was the expression of the eyes; large deep set, and dark, shining out form under finely arched eyebrows, they were indeed lumminous with the splendor of a pure and richly endowed soul.[32]

Also in 1883 Bishop Perce of New Orleans asked his former *Morning Star* editor to go on a lecture tour throughout the North to raise charitable funds for the diocese. The physically weak poet-priest reluctantly agreed and, by the end of the year, was in places like Baltimore, Boston, New York, and Philadelphia, being warmly greeted as the "Unreconstructed Ryan" and as a champion of common folks by the very same people he had detested all of his adult life. These people who came out to see the famous poet-priest of the South at every train station along the route were Democrats, especially Irishmen, who opposed the Republican administrations of Generals Grant, Hayes, and Garfield just as strongly as Ryan did. Overwhelmed by his positive reception in the North, Father Abram finally forgave the Northern Democrats for the death of his beloved brother. (Any such reconciliation with the Republicans would have been mutually unthinkable.) Back in 1879 the poet-priest had firmly turned down a request to include a poem for the Union dead in his first published collection, stating that he was not yet ready to communicate with "those people." Instead he included such a poem, "Requiem," under his own name, which had actually been written by a friend of his. By the spring of 1884, however, he was indeed ready for a change of heart. At the Decoration Day ceremony in Fond du Lac, Wisconsin, the Confederate veteran, surrounded by blue-clad Union veterans, recited his own poem, "Requiem For The Federal Dead."

> *Let all hatred end!*
> *From the bright golden shore*

They cry to the world,
Be brothers once more.

During the fall tour of 1884 Father Abram J. Ryan, the Southern Democrat, put in a good word for New York Governor S. Grover Cleveland, the successful Democratic nominee for President of the United States. Reconciliation with the North did not, however, detour Abram from writing more poems dedicated to the slain David. "In Memoriam" was composed twenty-one years after "In Memory of My Brother."

Thou art sleeping, brother, sleeping
In thy lonely battle grave;
Shadows o'er the past are creeping;
Death, the reaper, still is reaping,
Years have swept, and years are sweeping
Many a memory from my keeping,
But I'm waiting still, and weeping,
For my beautiful and brave.[33]

By August 1885 the strenuous series of Northern tours caused Father Abram's health to decline severely. He convalesced at the home of Mrs. Robert Harding in Danville, Kentucky. Here he worked on his own version of *The Life of Christ* and wrote his last poem.

Some day in the Spring,
When earth is fair and glad,
And sweet birds sing,
And fewest hearts are sad—
Shall I die then?

Knowing that the end was near, he transferred his residency to St. Boniface Monastery, where he died on Holy Thursday, April 24, 1886, at the age of forty-eight. Scholar, saint, parish priest, poet, editor, writer, preacher, orator, musician, unreconstructed philosopher, white supremist, Klansman, Democratic politician, uncompromising

Southern patriot, Confederate veteran. He had been all of these things in one brief lifetime. But more than anything else the man was a Rebel. In the end there had not been even a hint of personal scandal, no money, no property. His legacy was love of God and country. The coffin of Father Abram J. Ryan, wrapped in a huge Confederate battle flag, was shipped by train to Mobile, arriving on the afternoon of Easter Sunday and lying in state at St. Patrick's Cathedral all day Monday. Weeping common folks from all walks of life filed past to say good-bye to their beloved poet-priest who had appealed to their pride in defeat. On Tuesday morning a funeral appropriate for a head of state was attended by about four thousand people, including President and Mrs. Davis, along with hundreds of fully uniformed Confederate veterans. He was buried next to Rear Admiral Raphael Semmes, the most decorated sailor of the Confederate Navy. The Old South had paid last respects to one of its heroes, but tributes to Ryan would be bestowed for years to come.[34]

In July 1913 the city of Mobile erected a monument to the "Poet-Priest of the South," which stands in a square named after him at St. Francis Street and Springhill Avenue. On the monument there is an inscription:

The warrior's banner takes its flight
To greet the warrior's soul.

Similar monuments were raised in Augusta, New Orleans, Biloxi, and Louisville. The spirit and fame of the wandering priest spread throughout the South. In 1905 the school commission of the state of Georgia issued the pamphlet *Selections for the Observance of the Birth of General Robert E. Lee in the Schools of Georgia.* Not only was Ryan's "The Sword of Robert E. Lee" included, but it came with a set of instructions for reciting and pantomiming the poem. The Alabama Department of Education issued a similar booklet in 1907, featuring both "The Conquered Banner" and "The Sword of Robert E. Lee." When South Carolina's Lieutenant General Stephen D. Lee (no relation to the Lees of Virginia) was elected Commander-In-Chief of the United Confederate Veterans in 1904, he sent a letter to the leading educators of the South, urging them to have both famous Ryan poems formally memorized by all students.[35] A quarter of a century after his death the works of Father Abram J. Ryan were much better known than the poet-priest himself. Within another quarter of a century his name had been forgotten by most Southerners. Today very few Americans have ever heard of the man or his works.

The final resting place of Private David Ryan, a young trooper who rode with General John Hunt Morgan, has never been found.

NOTES

1. Msgr. Charles C. Boldrick, "His Story Runneth Thus." Paper read on January 19, 1972, to the Louisville Civil War Roundtable; Msgr. Oscar H. Lipscomb, "Ryan: His Life and Works." Paper read on April 4, 1972, before the Alabama Historical Association, Birmingham.

2. Thomas L. Connelly and Barbara L. Bellows, *God and General Longstreet* (Baton Rouge, 1982), pp. 1–38.

3. Msgr. H. J. Heagney, *Chaplain in Gray: Abraham Ryan* (New York, 1959); Tom J. Mills "Abraham J. Ryan," *Southern Bivouac*, vol. 2, no. 12, pp. 15–18; vol. 3, no. 1, pp. 21–25; and vol. 3, no. 2, pp. 11–13.
Author's Note: Heagney's undocumented work claims to be based on "records, wartime correspondence, and talks with many people who knew the poet-priest in their childhood." Not true. The Monsignor, a short-story author, simply made it up as he went along, text complete with intimate chit-chat between historical characters and fictitious characters. In the book Father Ryan was sent by President Davis to the Vatican on a diplomatic mission. Thus the author confused the poet-priest with Father John S. Bannon of the First Missouri Brigade. Ryan did not meet Davis until fifteen years after the war. In regard to the war itself, Heagney describes General Robert E. Lee as a mere figurehead who remained behind in Richmond during campaigns, leaving all real responsibilities to Lieutenant Generals Thomas J. Jackson and J. E. B. Stuart. The discredited Lieutenant General James Longstreet is not even mentioned. Army structure is totally muddled with corps, divisions, and even brigades all appearing as separate "armies."

4. Louis Joseph Maloof, "Abram J. Ryan, The Editor." Master's Thesis, University of Georgia. Athens: 1950, p. 12, Hargrett Rare Book and Manuscript Library; Cornelia Jean Crowley O'Connor, "Clarksville's Part in the Civil War." Immaculate Conception Church Dedication Book. Kathleen Welsh Wilson, editor. (Clarksville, Tennessee, 1980), p. 18.

5. Erwin Craighead, *Fact and Tradition* (Mobile, 1930), p. 231; Robert Sidney Douglas, *History of Southeast Missouri* (St. Louis, 1928), p. 194;

Oscar H. Lipscomb, "Some Unpublished Poems of Abram J. Ryan," *Alabama Historical Review*, vol. 25, no. 5 (July 1972), p. 164; *The Record* (Louisville), January 12, 1928.

6. Charles C. Broderick, "Father Abram J. Ryan: The Poet Priest of the Confederacy," *The Filson Club* (Louisville) *Historical Quarterly*, vol. 46, no. 3 (July, 1972), p. 205; Rev. J. P. Mc Key, (C.M.) *History of Niagara University* (New York, 1931), pp. 154–158; O'Connor, p. 18; *The Record* (Louisville), January 12, 1928; Register of The Barrens, 1843–1865, De Andreis Rosati Archives, vol. A12. Perryville, Missouri.

7. *The Record* (Louisville) November 28, 1907; John Rothensteiner, *History of the Archdiocese of St. Louis.* (St. Louis, 1928), p. 66; *Lasalle* (Illinois) *Tribune*, 20th Anniversary Souvenir Edition, July, 1911.

Author's Note: As a young man, Ryan identified himself as a Missourian; as a middle-aged man he identified himself as an Alabaman.

8. Editor, "Father Ryan, Poet-Priest of the Confederacy," *Missouri Historical Review*, (October 1941), pp. 62–63; Amelia Arnold Heidt, "Abram J. Ryan, Poet-Priest of the South," *United Daughters of the Confederacy Magazine*, (December 1948), vol. 11, no. 12 p. 16.

Author's Note: Ryan never once identified himself by ancestry; no contemporary ever referred to him as an Irishman.

9. Boldrick, p. 206; McKey, pp. 165–67; *The Record* (Louisville), November 14, 1907.

Author's Note: The poet-priest never directly disregarded the order of a lawful Church superior. He would, however, get on his horse and ride out of town, thereby putting himself in the jurisdiction of a different authority figure. In those days, the assignment of priests was a very loose process.

10. Ed Gleeson, *Rebel Sons of Erin* (Indianapolis, 1993), p. 277; McKey, p. 169; O'Connor, p. 19.

11. Rev. H. Germain Aiden, O.S.B., *Catholic Military and Navy Chaplains* (Washington, 1929), p. 49; Baptismal Register, St. Mary's Church, Peoria, Illinois, October 4, 1863; Benjamin J. Blied, *Catholics and the Civil War* (Milwaukee, 1945), p. 123.

12. Boldrick, p. 209; Gleeson, p. 277; Howard Merriwether Lovett, "Father Ryan of the South," *Commonwealth* magazine, vol. 10 (September 1929), p. 504; McKey, pp. 169–170.

13. "Army Period," Ryan Collection, Spring Hill (Kentucky) College Library, 1941.

14. Baptismal Register, St. Joseph's Church, Knoxville, April 2, 1865; Boldrick, p. 210; Lipscomb, p. 167; *The Register* (Mobile) October 9, 1927.

15. *Freeman's Journal* (New York, May 24, 1865); *Abram J. Ryan* (Mobile, 1879), p. 150; John Hannis Taylor, "Abram J. Ryan," *Library of Southern Literature* (New Orleans, 1909), vol. 10, p. 4623.

Author's Note: Included here are stanzas one, seven, and nine.

16. O'Connor, p. 22; *Nashville American*, June 26, 1910; Mildred Louise Rutherford, *The South in History and Literature* (New York ,1906), p. 477.

17. September 16, 1866, letter from Father Abram J. Ryan to Mrs. Hannah Murray Conroy, Conroy Collection, Immaculate Conception Church, Clarksville, Tennessee; O'Connor, pp. 21–23.

Author's Note: In 1872 Father Patrick Joseph Gleeson became the pastor of Clarksville's Immaculate Conception Church, formerly St. Mary's. Like Ryan's parents, Gleeson had been born in County Tipperary. He was the great-uncle of the author; that is, the older brother of the author's paternal grandfather. Some of P. J. Gleeson's writings about Reconstruction Tennessee are in the possession of Ed Gleeson.

18. Boldrick, p. 211; "Poems of Father Ryan," Abram J. Ryan Collection, Belmont (North Carolina) Abbey College, Archives.

19. Patricia L. Faust, ed., *Historical Times Illustrated: Encyclopedia of the Civil War* (New York, 1986), p. 649; Knight, Lucian Lamar, *Georgia's Landmarks, Memorials, and Legends* (Atlanta, 1914), p. 211; Maloof, pp. 56–57.

20. "Father Abram J. Ryan Memoirs," Augusta (Georgia) College Library; Abram J. Ryan, *The Banner of the South*, "Our Principles and Position." An editorial, March 21, 1868.

21. Abram J. Ryan, "The Importance of Education," *The Banner of the South*. An editorial, April 26, 1869.

22. Heidt, p. 18; Ryan, *Poems*, p. 19.

Author's Note: Included here are the first and last stanzas.

23. Boldrick, p. 212; Knight, p. 211; O'Connor, p. 23.

24. July 30, 1870, letter of Bishop Augustine Verot to Mr. Leopold T. Blume and to Mr. Patrick Walsh. Papers and Letters of Father Ryan, Abram J. Ryan Collection, Belmont (North Carolina) Abbey College, Archives.

Author's Note: The Reconstruction Klan was *not* anti-Catholic. The Indiana-based Klan of 1915–1925 *was* anti-Catholic above all else. Ryan was probably but not certainly Klan Grand Chaplain for most or all of his eleven years in Mobile. Apparently the poet-priest did not like trains and used them only when necessary. Like his dad, Ryan was a true wanderer, preferring to travel by horseback from town to town, sometimes taking weeks to go relatively short distances.

25. August 24, 1870, letter of Father Abram J. Ryan to Mr. Leopold T. Blume and to Mr. Patrick Walsh, Papers and Letters of Father Ryan, Abram J. Ryan Collection, Belmont (North Carolina) Abbey College, Archives.

26. *Courier-Journal* (Louisville), April 24, 1886; *The Register* (Mobile) October 9, 1927.

27. H. J. Heagney, "Recollections of Father Ryan," *Catholic World*, vol. 136 (January 1928), pp. 501–502; Lipscomb, p. 169; Mattie Thompson, *History of Barbour County, Alabama* (Eufaula, Alabama 1939); pp. 283–284.

28. Boldrick, p. 213; Heidt, p. 18; Maloof, pp. 191–92.

Author's Note: Pope Pius IX was a staunch theological and social conservative who had recognized the Southern Confederacy as a belligerent nation during The War Between the States. Pius' philosophy of life was very much compatible with Ryan's. He was followed in 1878 by the highly progressive labor priest, Pope Leo XIII, whose philosophy of life was not at all compatible with Ryan's. Like Abram Ryan and unlike Augustine Verot and Patrick Feehan, John Quinlan and J. D. Perce were Southern Nationalists. On September 20, 1863, at the Battle of Chickamauga, General Harvey Hill refused to salute or to even rise for his commanding general, Braxton Bragg, an action which would get him demoted from brevet lieutenant general (corps commander) down to major general (division commander). This belligerent West Point professional was the same man who, twenty years later, became choked with sentiment by Ryan's recitation at Lee's tomb.

29. *Ryan*, Taylor, p. 4625.

30. Bishop John Quinlan Papers, Notes after Retreat, September 15–20, 1881, Archives of the Diocese of Mobile; Lipscomb, p. 173; Allison E. Young, "How Father Ryan Died," *Southern Bivouac*, vol. 2, no. 3; p. 169.

31. Boldrick, p. 215; "The President and Father Ryan," The Delaney Family Collection, Belmont (North Carolina) Abbey College, Archives.

32. Charles W. Hubner, *Representative Southern Poets* (New York 1906), pp. 108–109.

33. Boldrick, pp. 215–216; McKey, pp. 171–172.

Author's Note: It is interesting to note that Ryan was present in New York City when the fateful "Rum, Romanism, and Rebellion" statement was made by a supporter of Republican presidential candidate, James G. Blaine. This represented a slur against the wets, Catholics, and Southerners of the Democratic party. The city's Irish-Catholic community was especially enraged. Blaine disavowed the statement much too late, narrowly losing the state of New York and consequently the election to Cleveland. To say, however, that Ryan helped to carry New York for Cleveland would be a considerable historical stretch. One thing, though, is for sure. The election of 1884 was the first time that the presidency was captured by an undeclared coalition of conservative Northern Catholics and conservative Southern Baptists. Ryan bridged that new coaltion better than any other single individual of the Nineteenth Century.

34. *Courier-Journal* (Louisville) April 23, 1886; O'Connor, p. 25; Thompson, p. 504; Young, p. 169.

Author's Note: Ryan led a spartan lifestyle, having few material possessions at the end of his life.

35. Thomas L. Connelly, *The Marble Man: Robert E. Lee and His Image in American Society* (Baton Rouge, 1972), p. 114; Heidt, p. 18; *The Record* (Louisville) May 31, 1900.

TENNESSEE IRISHMEN
IN CONFEDERATE SERVICE

BETTER THAN HALF A CENTURY AGO, Army of Tennessee historian
Stanley F. Horn brought forth an interesting theory and made
a strong case for it. The notion was that the state of Tennessee never
really seceded from the Federal Union. Instead, Governor Isham G.
Harris personally seceded and took the state with him. There is a lot
to be said for this proposition. Prior to the hostilities at Fort Sumter,
the voting men of Tennessee, in a nonbinding popular referendum,
overwhelmingly supported union. The day after Sumter fell, however,
President Abraham Lincoln made a rare political mistake in judgment
and called upon Tennesseans to help raise seventy-five thousand volunteers for Federal service. Harris seized the moment to shift sympa-
thy toward secession. The governor's argument was that the President
was a bully, forcing the men of the Volunteer State to do something
that they did not want to do. Harris' efforts won out when the state
legislature in Nashville passed the Ordinance of Secession on June 10,
1861. Tennessee was the tenth of the eleven states to join the Southern Confederacy, followed only by Arkansas.

Governor Harris did not wait until June 10 to prepare for war.
Beginning on April 15, he began to raise volunteer companies for pro-
Southern state militia service, properly drilled units that could readily
be transferred to the Confederate Army. In an attempt to cover the
entire population base of the state, Harris expressed the intention of
raising thirty Irish companies to be formed into three full regiments,
which would then become an "Irish Brigade" of three thousand officers and men. A regiment of ten companies each was to come from the
three state military districts—West Tennessee, Middle Tennessee, and
East Tennessee. This ambitious plan came up sixteen hundred officers and men short, and so the original idea had to be abandoned. The
only complete success occurred in Middle Tennessee, where four Irish
settlements from four different counties turned out a full regiment of
ten companies. Seven companies were raised in West Tennessee, all
from the town of Memphis and surrounding Shelby County. One

undersized company was squeezed out of the pro-Union mountains of East Tennessee.

The eighteen companies of some fourteen hundred effectives represented an accomplishment in itself, considering that pro-Confederate Irish immigrants made up only a small percentage of the state's male population. Eighteen was the most green-flag Irish companies organized in any of the Southern states. (A green flag indicated that the men identified themselves as Irish.) Louisiana, however, provided the Confederacy with fewer but larger green-flag companies. In numbers, therefore, Tennessee ranked second (ahead of Missouri and Kentucky but behind Louisiana) in Irish immigrants and sons of Irish immigrants in Southern green-flag units. It should be noted that hundreds of other Irish Tennesseans served as individuals in units without green flags. Included among these were about 250 Irish-Americans listed on the muster rolls of the Twenty-First Tennessee Infantry, about one-third of all officers and men, mostly native-born Presbyterians and Methodists of Scotch-Irish descent. Although the Twenty-First was not a green-flag regiment, Irish-sounding names represented the majority on the rolls of D and E Companies. Many Irishmen and Irish-Americans could also be found in two of the companies (C and F) of the One Hundred-Fifty-Fourth Senior (formerly state militia) Tennessee Infantry, as well as in the C Company of the Watson Artillery Battalion. All five of the predominantly Irish companies without green flags were from Memphis, Shelby County.

The full green-flag regiment from Middle Tennessee was the Tenth Tennessee Infantry, a four-year combat unit that participated in most of the western campaigns, a strongly Catholic regiment with a number of Protestant commissioned officers. Three companies of non-Irish from Memphis were added to the seven companies of Memphis Irishmen, becoming one of two Confederate regiments designated as the Second Tennessee Infantry. This particular Second Tennessee was a non-green-flag regiment consisting mostly of native-born and Irish-born Episcopalians with a single company (F) of Irish-born Catholics. One of the most obscure green-flag Irish units in American military history has to be B Company, Third Confederate Battalion Engineer Corps, Department of East Tennessee, a small unit of noncombatants composed almost exclusively of County Clare-born Catholics. Like many of their Union Irish counterparts in the western theatre of operations, the story of the Tennessee Irish Confederates has never previously been told.

TENNESSEE IRISHMEN IN GREEN-FLAG COMPANIES
   10th Tenn. Inf. (10 companies, Nashville area).
   2nd Tenn. Inf. (Walker's, 7 companies, Memphis area).
   B Company, 3rd Conf. Batt. Engineers (Knoxville area).
   Total = 18 Companies of about 1,400 Effectives.

TENNESSEE IRISHMEN IN COMPANIES WITHOUT GREEN FLAGS
   21st Tenn. Inf. (D, E Companies, Memphis area).
   154th Senior Tenn. Inf. (C, F Companies, Memphis area).
   Reinforced Watson Louisiana Battery (C Company, Memphis area).
   Total = 5 Companies of about 400 Effectives.

PART I

MIDDLE TENNESSEE IRISHMEN IN

CONFEDERATE SERVICE

REBEL SONS OF ERIN: TENTH TENNESSEE INFANTRY

DESCRIBED BY ARMY OF TENNESSEE HISTORIAN Thomas Lawrence Connelly as "one of the most colorful outfits in the entire Confederacy," the Tenth Tennessee Infantry Regiment (Irish) was mustered into the Tennessee Home Guards (State Militia) on May 29, 1861, at Fort Donelson, Tennessee.[1] The Tenth consisted mainly of Irish immigrants and the sons of Irish immigrants from the four Middle Tennessee towns of Nashville (seven companies), Clarksville (one company), McEwen (one company), and downstate Pulaski (one company). Confederate regiments from Louisiana, Tennessee, Missouri, and Kentucky posted some Irish companies, but only in the Tenth Tennessee were all ten companies predominantly Irish.

The divisions and boundaries of modern Ireland did not exist in 1861. Most of the men came from seven of the twenty-three counties that comprise the three southern provinces (modern Republic of Ireland); some of the men came from the Ulster province (modern Northern Ireland). A majority of these Irishmen were Catholics; a highly visible minority, sometimes characterized as "Scotch-Irish" or "Anglo-Irish," were Protestants.[2] There was, however, not a single word of friction recorded in any of the regimental accounts concerning religion or nationalism. The regimental colors that the Irishmen proudly guarded had a green background with a gold harp. The inscription read: "Sons of Erin; Where Glory Awaits You."[3]

The Tenth Tennessee Irishmen, mostly common laborers and farmers, had been the militiamen who had done much of the construction work at Fort Donelson on the Cumberland River and Fort Henry on the Tennessee River. After three months of militia service in the Tennessee Home Guards, the Middle Tennessee Irishmen were mustered into regular Confederate service at Fort Henry, Tennessee on September 1, 1861, as the Tenth Tennessee Infantry Regiment (Irish), Confederate States Volunteers. The Irish regiment consisted of 720 officers and men, plus five noncombatants, all from the Tennessee counties of Davidson (town of Nashville), Montgomery (village of Clarksville), Humphries (hamlet of McEwen), Houston (hamlet of Erin), and Giles (village of Pulaski).

During the naval bombardment at Fort Henry, February 4–6, 1862, the "Sons of Erin" participated in two brief skirmishes with Federal cavalrymen—at Panther Creek and on the Charlotte Road. The Irish regiment then served as the Confederate rear guard during the evacuation from Fort Henry to Fort Donelson, a march that covered twelve miles. Colonel Adolphus Heiman, a Prussian-born Nashville engineer with a distinguished Mexican War record, had been the original commanding officer. When Heiman was given brigade responsibility at Fort Henry, regimental command passed to Lieutenant Colonel Randal William McGavock, a likable six-foot two-inch red-haired Nashville-born Tennessean of prominent Presbyterian Scotch-Irish background.[4] Randal McGavock, like his uncle of the same name, had once been mayor of Nashville.

When Fort Henry fell on February 6, General Albert Sidney Johnston, commanding the Confederate Department of the West, sent four of his brigadiers into Dover, Tennessee, near Fort Donelson to eventually command a force of six small brigades, including Heiman's three regiments. By seniority of rank the four Southern generals were John B. Floyd of Virginia, Gideon J. Pillow of Tennessee, Simon B. Buckner of Kentucky, and Bushrod R. Johnson of Nashville, the scholarly Ohio-born Quaker who had received his promotion to brigadier a mere two weeks earlier. Their assignment was to defend the critical Cumberland garrison protecting Nashville against Brigadier General U. S. Grant's Union army corps of Major General Henry Halleck's Department of Missouri, a reinforced command of three full infantry divisions and a Navy squadron of seven gunboats.

General Bushrod Johnson's division at Fort Donelson was deployed in the middle of the three-mile Confederate line. His command was formed from the two Fort Henry infantry brigades of Heiman and Colonel Joseph Drake of Mississippi.[5] Facing Johnson's division across the valley was the all-Illinois Federal First Division of three brigades commanded by Brigadier General John A. McClernand, an ambitious glory-seeking Southern Illinois politician. Heiman's brigade, reinforced by units from General Pillow's command, was posted in the center of the defensive line between the troops of Colonel Drake on the left (east) and General Buckner on the right (west). It consisted of the Tenth, Thirtieth, Fortieth, Forty-Second, Forty-Eighth, and Fifty-Third Tennessee regiments, plus the Twenty-Seventh Alabama and the four-gun Tennessee battery of Captain Frank Maney.[6]

With the Confederate infantry facing south and away from the river, the Tenth Tennessee's trenches were dug into the top right (west) side of a detached V-shaped ridge, soon to be known as Heiman's Hill, near the highest point on the Confederate line. The Irish regiment formed the German colonel's far right wing, exactly midway between the fort's stockade and the town of Dover. The

Irishmen were engaged in only one land action during the Dover campaign, but it proved to be a monumental success—thanks to a huge
mistake in judgment by McClernand.

By Thursday, February 13, Heiman, the skillful Nashville engineer, had his reinforced brigade dug in deep atop the V-shaped ridge.[7]
To the left of the Tenth Tennessee were the rest of Heiman's regiments, the Fifty-Third Tennessee and the Twenty-Seventh Alabama
deployed front center at the point of the V, with the Fortieth Tennessee equidistant from the Irish regiment near the top of the ridge's left
side. Above the Twenty-Seventh Alabama, on the left side of the V,
was the Forty-Eighth Tennessee. Above the Fifty-Third Tennessee, to
the right of the V, was Maney's battery. Between the Tenth Tennessee and the Fortieth Tennessee, at the center of the peak, a few companies of the Forty-Second and Thirtieth Tennessee regiments were
held in reserve.

At 9:30 A.M. Maney's gunners knocked a wheel off one of the
Union artillery wagons. Responding irrationally to the action,
McClernand, disregarding Grant's orders to hold his position, detached four infantry regiments from his division and instructed them
to take Heiman's Hill with the intent of silencing Maney. The Illinois
general made no reconnaissance of the area and took all morning get-
ting his troops in place, in full view of all the Southerners on the ridge.
The Union detachment consisted of the Seventeenth, Forty-Fifth,
Forty-Eighth, and Forty-Ninth Illinois regiments, commanded by
Colonel Isham Haynie of the Forty-Eighth.[8] McClernand began his
reckless, piecemeal assault at 12:45 P.M. by charging Heiman's left
flank with Colonel William Morrison and the Forty-Ninth Illinois.

Heiman responded by advancing a battalion of the Forty-Second
Tennessee up to the rifle pits to reinforce the Fifty-Third Tennessee
and the Twenty-Seventh Alabama. The Illinoisans of the Forty-Ninth
were raked with heavy fire and forced off the hill. Haynie advanced
companies of the Seventeenth and Forty-Eighth regiments from his
skirmish line and launched a second wave against Maney's battery and
the Fifty-Third Tennessee, again spearheaded by companies of the
Forty-Ninth Illinois. Morrison was, however, seriously wounded
within a few minutes and the Illinois Federals fell back into the woods

in considerable confusion. McClernand ordered Haynie to launch a third wave with his reserve regiment, the Forty-Fifth Illinois, mostly lead-miners from Grant's hometown of Galena.[9]

As the Illinoisans of the Forty-Ninth, Forty-Eighth, and Seventeenth filed back into the woods in a state of disorder, the Forty-Fifth got pushed from the Union right to center and then to the left of center. The only opening for an attack lay in the woods in front of Heiman's Hill at the west end of the battlefield—Union left, Confederate right—below those rifle pits where McGavock and his Irishmen were posted.[10] While the battle raged on the east end of the field between the Fifty-Third Tennessee and the Forty-Ninth Illinois, McGavock skillfully divided his regiment into two infantry battalions and a sharpshooters detachment.

On McGavock's left were elements of five companies under Episcopalian, Irish-born Captain (later lieutenant colonel) Samuel M. Thompson of Nashville. On McGavock's right, which was the extreme right of Heiman's line, were elements of the other five companies under Catholic Tennessee-born Major (later colonel) William Grace, a six-foot-three-and-a-half-inch giant, also of Nashville. Behind McGavock's line, at the highest point of the ridge behind some trees, were the marksmen of youthful Catholic Irish-born Captain (later lieutenant colonel) John G. O'Neill of McEwen, assisted by Catholic Irish-born Sergeant (later captain) John L. Prendergast of Clarksville, and by Catholic Irish-born Corporal (later first lieutenant) Thomas "Long Tom" Connor of Nashville.[11]

The Federals, with an artillery advantage, had already knocked out two of Maney's four guns and continued to pound Heiman's Hill. At 1:25 drummers of the Forty-Fifth Illinois beat out the rally. As the gunsmoke cleared below, the Tennessee Irishmen could see images of battle below them. Leading the blue-clad columns was a distinguished-looking officer on horseback, Swiss-born Colonel John E. Smith of Galena, a watchmaker.[12] Leaving some of his companies on the skirmish line, the Swiss colonel led a detachment of lead-miners down and then up the incline. At the base of the hill one of the advancing infantrymen looked straight up and noticed two colorful sights high above.[13]

There was a big, mounted, red-haired officer in a red-and-gold-trimmed gray uniform with a green feather in the red lining of his gray hat, pointing a sword toward him that flashed in the Tennessee afternoon sun. The Confederate officer was Randal McGavock. The other sight that the Illinois soldier noticed even higher on the ridge was a kelly-green flag with white shamrocks flapping the in the wind.[14] This was McGavock's own personal colors. For many of the attackers, those were the last two sights they would ever see.

At the same time that McGavock ordered the Irishmen to open fire, Heiman motioned to Maney to have canister loaded into his remaining two pieces. A murderous storm of musketry and canister swept the right end of Heiman's Hill. The front line of the Union third wave went down in a heap. Private Wilbur Crummer of the Forty-Fifth Illinois described the Confederate spray of lead as "terrific . . . Presently the balls began to sing about our heads: Zip, ping, ping," was what he recalled in his memoirs.[15] Some of the Galena lead-miners remained on the skirmish line, while others held onto the lower cliffs and fired up. Still others continued to ascend the ridge, veering from their center to left, but McGavock adjusted his right flank in toward the invaders, who then became pinned down by O'Neill's sharpshooters.

In spite of McGavock's firepower, a small unit of the Illinoisans made it to the breastworks in front of Thompson's command, just to the left center of the Tenth Tennessee line. Because the angle of fire was so severe for the Federals closest to the wall, they were forced to continue their advance with fixed bayonets. Sergeant (later second lieutenant) John Ames, the ferocious, dark-skinned, Catholic and Irish-born drillmaster of A Company, from McEwen, looking somewhat like a Mexican bandit with several weapons tucked inside his belt, fired one of his revolvers point blank into the face of an enemy soldier on the wall, and the man's head exploded with blood and tissue and bone splinters splattering all over the thorns and prickly branches.[16]

Federal drummers pounded out the beat of retreat as Smith and his assault force retired to their skirmish line. The air was filled with the smell of powder as McClernand's artillery continued to pound the earth in front of the Confederate trenches. Exposed to enemy fire from gunners and sharpshooters in the valley, McGavock and Tennessee-born, Presbyterian, Scotch-Irish Captain Saint Clare Morgan rode up and down the line warning the Irishmen to have their weapons re-loaded.[17] In less than two minutes other companies of the Forty-Fifth Illinois charged McGavock's position, reinforced by a small detach-ment of the Forty-Ninth Illinois, consisting of some of the men who had already seen action at the other end of the line. Smith ordered his troops up from the left end of his skirmish line, McGavock's far right. This would prove to be yet another Union tactical mistake, although Smith had no way of knowing it. What followed was Smith's second and last wave of Haynie's third and last wave of the Battle of Erin Hollow.

Standing high atop the breastworks on the ridge's far right side, directing the fire of his battalion with the wave of his sword, was the gigantic figure of Grace, an outstanding Irish-American combat of-ficer.[18] The mere sight of Grace was enough to slow down even the most gallant of the Illinoisans. The falling bodies from the last assault force stampeded their comrades down the incline and into the woods. "My regiment behaved nobly and it was as much as I could do to keep them in the pits, they were so anxious to get out and charge them," McGavock reported.[19] According to the testimony of Jimmy Doyle, the Tennessee son of Irish-Catholic immigrants, the Irishmen whose enthusiasm had to be contained by McGavock were led by the Catho-lic, Irish-born Fitzgerald twins, Privates Morris and William, a pair of very pugnacious soldiers.[20]

A Confederate counterassault proved unnecessary when Federal gunners in the valley hoisted up a flag of truce-cease-fire. Heiman rode up and down the line to the shouts of the victorious Southerners. Blue-clad dead and wounded covered the landscape. The three waves of McClernand's folly of February 13, 1862, had lasted fifty-five min-utes, ending in a crushing defeat. In the last fifteen of those minutes, Smith and his lead miners had twice unsuccessfully contested the po-sition of McGavock and his Tennessee Irishmen.

Shortly after two, with the Union stretcher-bearers rapidly ap-proaching the battle area, the woods in front of Heiman's Hill caught on fire as a result of the combination of exploding shells with dry, mild weather. Cries of panic and pain rose up from the ravine, soon to be replaced by coughing and choking. The wounded Illinoisans were in grave danger. A Union emergency field hospital was hastily set up near Erin Hollow Creek for victims of both gunshots and burns. In an act of great honor, representing everything that was good and decent about the gentlemen of the Old South, Colonels Heiman and McGavock assembled volunteers for a rescue operation.[21] At least two Illinoisans were saved by an all-Tennessee team of workers. Tenth Tennessee heroes included Father Henry Vincent Browne, the Dominican priest who was regimental chaplain and Catholic Irish-born Private (later corporal) Michael Carney.[22]

Haynie reported 122 killed, about 200 wounded, and another 100 missing in action (later updated to almost 200 missing) for a casualty rate of about forty percent of those engaged, all in less than an hour's fight. The Forty-Fifth Illinois suffered 16 killed, about 35 wounded, and several others missing, most or all of whom were victims of the Tenth Tennessee, all in about fifteen minutes.[23] Heiman reported a total of about 40 losses in his entire reinforced brigade, less than two percent of those engaged, and none at all for the Tenth Tennessee.[24] Erin Hollow was to be the first of four skirmishes in which the Sons of Erin inflicted a total of about 200 losses on the enemy while sustaining zero losses themselves in those four actions! The legend of the "Bloody Tenth" has been misunderstood—it was the Federals making the mad dashes against the Tennessee Irishmen who got bloodied.

At the major land action of Saturday, February 15, Heiman's brigade was kept in reserve on the V-shaped ridge as a buffer between the Union First Division and the Union Second and Third Divisions. As a result the Tenth was not engaged on that day, which featured another series of Confederate successes. On the following morning, however, after incompetents Floyd and Pillow had left their command behind, Buckner had no choice but to surrender to Grant. McGavock and his entire regiment were captured and sent to three Federal prisons—Camp Douglas in Chicago, Camp Chase in Columbus, Ohio, and Fort Warren in Boston. Twenty-two of the Irish lads died in confinement, all at Douglas.[25] The prisoners were exchanged in September and only about half the Irishmen reenlisted.

The Tenth Tennessee was reorganized at Clinton, Mississippi, on October 2, 1862, with 383 officers and men present for duty.[26] On November 16 Adolphus Heiman died of disease and Randal McGavock was promoted to full colonel.[27] The Sons of Erin were assigned to the brigade of Brigadier General John Gregg of Texas, who had been McGavock's roommate at Fort Warren. Gregg's command was part of Lieutenant General John C. Pemberton's Department of Mississippi, Tennessee, and Louisiana. President Jefferson Davis had given Pemberton the awesome responsibility of defending the critically important Confederate garrison at Vicksburg on the Mississippi.

During Grant's unsuccessful assault against Vicksburg in December, the Irish lads of the Tenth were held in reserve at Chickasaw Bluffs before going into winter quarters at Port Hudson on the Mississippi just above Baton Rouge, Louisiana.[28] Grant, with nine infantry divisions, began a spring offensive against Vicksburg in April, 1863. In early May Pemberton sent Gregg's brigade up to protect the Mississippi state capital of Jackson, thirty-five miles due east of Vicksburg. McGavock and his Irishmen, along with the rest of Gregg's troops, arrived by train on May 11. The Texan decided to defend the approaches to Jackson by marching his brigade twelve miles southwest to the tiny hamlet of Raymond. During the late evening and early morning hours of May 11–12 the Confederates dug entrenchments out of the wooded hills just south of Raymond, thereby blocking the only two roads into Jackson.

Sickness and desertions had decreased Colonel McGavock's command to 254 effectives, mostly men from Davidson, Montgomery, and Humphries counties, a few from Giles County. General Gregg consolidated the Tenth with Lieutenant Colonel James J. Turner's Thirtieth Tennessee of 171 effectives, mostly men from Summer and Robertson counties, some from Macon and Smith counties, giving McGavock a total of 425 officers and men present for duty, including himself.[29] In addition to McGavock's Tenth/Thirtieth Tennessee consolidated regiment, Gregg's infantry brigade consisted of the Seventh Texas regiment, the First Tennessee Battalion, and the Third, Forty-First, and Fiftieth Tennessee regiments, a total of 2,730 men.

Grant sent his Federal Seventeenth Corps, commanded by Major General James B. McPherson, west to capture Jackson. This command had three divisions of Westerners from Ohio, Indiana, Illinois, and Missouri. Not sure about the size of the Confederate force in front of him, McPherson kept his first two divisions in reserve and advanced with the three brigades of his Third Division under Major General John A. Logan. The brigades were commanded by Brigadier Generals Elias S. Dennis, John D. Stevenson, and John E. Smith, the Swiss watchmaker from Galena. On Tuesday morning, May 12, Logan marched his troops northeast up the Utica Road. At ten both sides exchanged heavy artillery and sharpshooters fire.

Gregg's right flank, on the western end of the field at the Utica Road, was held down by Colonel Hiram B. Grandbury and the Texas regiment supported on a second line by elements of Colonel Robert Farquharson's Forty-First Tennessee. Gregg's center, between the two roads, was held down by Colonel Calvin H. Walker and the Third Tennessee, supported on a second line by the rest of the Forty-First. Gregg's left flank, on the eastern end of the field at the Gallatin Road, was held down by Lieutenant Colonel Thomas W. Beaumont and the Fiftieth Tennessee supported on a second line by Colonel Randal W. McGavock and the Tenth/Thirtieth Tennessee consolidated.[30] Behind the Confederate line to the north, on a higher hill, was the three-gun Missouri battery of Captain Hiram M. Bledsoe, supported by Major Stephen H. Colm's small First Tennessee Battalion. In front of the Confederate line to the south was a shallow stream called Fourteen-Mile Creek in a heavily wooded area.

Logan kept Stevenson's brigade in reserve near the Gallatin Road and assaulted Grandbury's position near the Utica Road with the brigades of Dennis and Smith, spearheaded by the Twentieth Ohio and Twenty-Third Indiana. By noon the Federals had crossed the creek and were prepared to establish a new line in a clearing of the woods when Gregg personally led a counterassault with his own original regiment, the Seventh Texas, supported by the Third and Forty-First Tennessee, all of which chased the surprised Ohioans and Hoosiers back south of the creek.[31] Logan personally counterassaulted Gregg's counterassault with some of his rested regiments and re-established the

THE BATTLE OF RAYMOND, MISS.

THURSDAY, MAY 12, 1863 — 1 P.M. POSITIONS

Union line in the woods north of the creek. At one, Gregg ordered
Beaumont into the fight to be followed by McGavock after Beaumont
became engaged.

Using the hill he held as an observation post, Beaumont saw enemy columns in the distance coming at him in large numbers. It was
the three regiments of Stevenson's makeshift brigade. Overprudently,
Beaumont took the battlefield initiative and withdrew his regiment up
the Gallatin Road, leaving a four-hundred-yard gap between
Farquharson and McGavock.[32] Even worse, the courier of the Fiftieth
Tennessee couldn't locate either Gregg or McGavock. By 1:30 Logan
had put his numerical strength to good use with his two brigades of
Dennis and J. E. Smith on the Utica Road, leaving only a few compa-
nies of the three defending Confederate regiments (Seventh Texas,
Third Tennessee, Forty-First Tennessee) clinging to the road.

With Logan, Dennis, and Smith heavily engaged with Grandbury,
Walker and Farquharson on the Union left, Confederate right,
McPherson ordered Stevenson to take the Gallatin Road on the eastern end of his line. When Gregg realized that Beaumont was not
where he was supposed to be, he ordered McGavock to stop
Stevenson.[33] McGavock deployed his 424 Tennesseans on the south
end of a bald hill near the Gallatin Road, with the Tenth up front,
supported on a second line by the Thirtieth. As Stevenson's lead regiment, the Seventh U.S. Missouri, consisting of Irishmen from St.
Louis, approached the base of the hill, McGavock signaled for his
Tennessee Irishmen to charge.[34] The Scotch-Irish colonel was killed
instantly with a single shot to the heart. It was two o'clock.

Lieutenant Colonel William Grace led the Tennessee assault force
down the hill without the benefit of an artillery cover. The Catholic
Nashville Irishmen became locked in a savage hand-to-hand combat
with the Catholic St. Louis Irishmen. In this first stage of the engagement, Tennessee-born, Baptist Captain George A. Diggons and Captain John L. Prendergast were both seriously wounded by shell frag-
ments. Presbyterian, Irish-born Private John McElroy stayed on his
feet in spite of being wounded three times by musketry fire. Ames, the
drillmaster, and Catholic, Irish-born Sergeant James Hyde were both
killed by multiple gunshots.[35]

After about twenty minutes of this carnage, the Seventh U.S. Missouri was reinforced by some of the companies of the Thirty-Second Ohio. Realizing that he was outnumbered, Turner, then commanding the consolidated regiment, organized a retirement back north to a heavily wooded ridge near the Gallatin Road, a position which could be defended. During the second stage of the engagement, 2:30 to 3, Grace and his Irishmen ambushed a single company of the Thirty-Second Ohio, coming off the wooded hill to thirty steps in front of them and routing their color guard. The Fitzgerald brothers, filled with rage and with bayonets extended, fought like demons to avenge McGavock's killing.[36]

At about three Turner detached A Company of his Irish regiment as a sharpshooter unit consisting of some forty-five Irishmen, mostly Irish-born farmers from McEwen.[37] As the commanding officer of the detachment, Captain John G. O'Neill deployed his marksmen at the highest point on the ridge, behind a farm and some trees. At the lower levels, Turner strung out a double line of skirmishers. Almost immediately other companies of Stevenson's brigade (Seventh U.S. Missouri, Eighty-First Illinois, Thirty-Second Ohio), emerged from a forest with their skirmishers advancing at a run to a ravine near the base of O'Neill's Hill. (This third and last stage of the engagement was remembered by the survivors of the Tenth Tennessee as the Battle of O'Neill's Hill.)

The action lasted something less than thirty minutes and concluded when the Federals crawled back to the safety of their woods after having suffered heavy casualties. Turner credited O'Neill's detachment with much of the damage.[38] Twelve of the invaders (seven from the Seventh U.S. Missouri and five from the Eighty-First Illinois) were so pinned down by O'Neill that they were forced to surrender to Grace.[39] By four o'clock, however, Logan's three brigades had overwhelmed the lone Confederate brigade and Gregg was forced to withdraw north and east of Raymond. By five McPherson began to occupy the Mississippi hamlet. Two days later, due to insufficient Confederate reinforcements, Jackson fell to Grant.

The action around O'Neill's Hill at Raymond, like the action around Heiman's Hill at Erin Hollow, lasted only fifteen or twenty minutes and produced the same results—many Federal losses, but no losses for the Sons of Erin. During their entire one-and-a-half-hour engagement at the Battle of Raymond, the Tenth Tennessee suffered eight killed, thirty-five wounded, and nine captured or missing, for a total loss of fifty-two men, twenty percent of those engaged, bringing the number of regimental effectives down to 190.[40] Colonel William Grace and his remaining Irishmen were assigned to General Braxton Bragg's Army of Tennessee, arriving in North Georgia on September 17, 1863, just in time to participate in three days of heavy fighting at the Battle of Chickamauga.

During the Tullahoma campaign of June 23 to September 7, 1863, Major General William S. Rosecrans, commanding the Union Army of the Cumberland, maneuvered Bragg completely out of East Tennessee without having to fight a major battle. With Chattanooga occupied by the Federals, the important Confederate production center at Atlanta was wide open to invasion. For the purpose of securing Atlanta, Bragg was ordered to push Rosecrans out of Chattanooga. To accomplish this task, the Richmond War Department sent two crack divisions of Lieutenant General James Longstreet's First Corps west to reinforce Bragg.

Rosecrans and Bragg were both bivouacked in North Georgia, about nine miles southwest of Chattanooga, along the West Chickamauga Creek. The Lafayette Road, running north-south in and out of Chattanooga, was the key to victory for both armies. Bragg's objective for Friday, September 18, was to advance west and cross the creek in front of Rosecrans' line along the road. If the Confederates could entrench in this position, they would be able to launch an assault on the following day and capture the critical road which led back up to Chattanooga.

Colonel William Grace and the Tenth Tennessee, in Gregg's brigade of Bushrod Johnson's division, were deployed at the north end of the battlefield, where Bragg had ordered Johnson to advance westward and secure Reed's Bridge on the West Chickamauga.[41] A Federal detachment of three dismounted cavalry regiments, commanded by Irish-born Colonel R. H. G. Minty, was stationed on Pea Vine Ridge, a hill about five hundred yards east of the bridge, in a position to block the Confederate approaches. After stubborn resistance, the Northern troopers were driven off the hill and over the bridge. During the afternoon action around Pea Vine Ridge and Reed's Bridge, the Sons of Erin were detached as infantry support for the First Missouri Confederate Battery of Gregg's brigade. O'Neill and his sharpshooters poured a heavy fire into the enemy from both flanks of the three Missouri guns.[42] This was the third skirmish of less than a half hour's duration in which the Tennessee Irishmen inflicted several casualties while sustaining none themselves.

With Gregg's brigade as the vanguard of Johnson's division, the Southerners crossed the bridge and marched south to a granary compound called Lee and Gordon's Mills, where there was some night skirmishing. It was here that First Lieutenant Theodore Kelsey, the Episcopalian, Irish-born courier of the Tenth, was killed by a Federal sharpshooter. Kelsey was replaced by Episcopalian, Irish-born First Lieutenant Robert Paget Seymour, an Anglo-Irish veteran of the British Army.[43]

Saturday, September 19 (first official day of battle), was one of the most chaotic twenty-four hours in American military history. Both Rosecrans and Bragg lost track of events, while many of their subordinates took the initiative, resulting in a continuous series of disorganized assaults and counter-assaults along the Lafayette Road, all of which left both armies in almost the same position at the end of the day. At 4 P.M. Gregg went forward to reconnoiter the road and was wounded.[44] His senior colonel, Cyrus A. Sugg of the Fiftieth Tennessee, took command of the brigade. Shortly after Gregg fell, Major General John Bell Hood, commanding a detached corps of two divisions, ordered two of the brigades of Johnson's division on his extreme left flank to assault the Federals in front of him to the west of the road. The charging Southern force consisted of the brigades of Sugg and Colonel John S. Fulton, while the defending Northern force consisted of the two brigades of Union Brigadier General Jefferson C. Davis' division.

In the confusion of some dense woods, four of Johnson's regiments got cut off from the main assault force. These units were the Tenth, Thirtieth, and Forty-First Tennessee regiments of Sugg and the Seventeenth Tennessee regiment of Fulton.[45] The result was a makeshift brigade temporarily commanded by Grace, the only full colonel of the detachment. It was at this time that Catholic, Irish-born Captain William Sweeney, commanding D Company of the Tenth, was killed in action.[46] When Davis' division was reinforced by troops from Union Brigadier General Thomas Wood's division, Johnson, Fulton, Sugg, and Grace were forced to withdraw to their original position east of the Lafayette Road. The two "armed mobs" ended the slugfest around 6:30 P.M.

On Sunday, September 20 (second official day of battle) the Irishmen of the Tenth Tennessee participated in two heavy engagements, at Dyer's Farm and on Steedman's Hill, their heaviest actions of the war. In the morning Rosecrans had accidentally created a huge hole in the Union line and Longstreet had accidentally poured five divisions into it, including Johnson's. Shortly before noon Grace and his Sons of Erin raced westward across the undefended Lafayette Road, capturing a surprised enemy battery in a wheat field.[47] Just to the west was the Dyer family farmhouse, where a wooded hill was held down by a small detachment of German gunners from the First U.S. Missouri Battery supported by two companies of German infantrymen from the Second U.S. Missouri, a force commanded by First Lieutenant Gustavus Schueler. When Johnson ordered Sugg to take the hill, Grace and the Tennessee Irishmen climbed the backside and engaged the enemy in hand-to-hand combat, forcing the Missouri Germans to surrender.[48] Grace, however, lost two of his top combat officers; Lieutenant Colonel Samuel Thompson was permanently disabled and Captain Morgan was killed.[49]

By mid-afternoon the only Federals still on the field were the troops of Major General George H. Thomas' Fourteenth Corps, reinforced by two brigades of Major General Gordon Granger's Reserve Corps. Thomas was posted on a series of ridges at the northern end of the battlefield near the Snodgrass family farmhouse, a position known as Horseshoe Ridge, which was accessible to McFarland's Gap of Missionary Ridge, an escape route to Chattanooga. At 2:30 Bushrod Johnson, with four of Longstreet's brigades including Fulton's, attacked the Union position but was forced back with heavy losses. An hour later, when Johnson was reinforced by Sugg's six regiments including the Tenth Tennessee, Thomas responded with Granger's troops, commanded by Brigadier General James B. Steedman.[50] The brigade commanders of the improvised Union division were Colonels Walter C. Whitaker and John G. Mitchell.

Grace's Confederate Irishmen advanced from their position on Vittetoe's Hill to the southern end of a low hill just west of the southernmost knob of Horseshoe Ridge, soon to be known as Steedman's Hill. During the twenty minutes of desperate fighting at the crest of the low ridge, Sugg's second line, consisting of the Tenth and Thirtieth Tennessee regiments, was forced off the hill by Lieutenant Colonel Darius Warner's One-Hundred-Thirteenth Ohio regiment of Mitchell's brigade.[51] Episcopalian Anglo-Irish First Lieutenant John D. Winston and four enlisted men of the Irish regiment were killed or mortally wounded in this action.[52] When Grace's horse was shot out from under him during the evacuation, Lieutenant Seymour dragged the colonel up onto his own mount; and so even though the Nashville Irish-American Catholic was seriously injured, he avoided capture, thanks to the efforts of his Irish-born Protestant courier.[53]

By evening the Federals, out of ammunition, withdrew through McFarland's Gap back up to Chattanooga. In three days at Chickamauga the Tenth Tennessee suffered 11 killed, 37 wounded, two of whom were captured and later died at Camp Douglas, for combined losses of 48 out of 190, twenty-five percent of those engaged.[54] The Confederate tactical victory was, however, turned into a strategic defeat when Bragg occupied the northern ends of Lookout Mountain and Missionary Ridge but failed to pursue the defeated Rosecrans into Chattanooga.

At the November 25 Battle of Missionary Ridge, the Sons of Erin, with 104 effectives and with Major O'Neill replacing the injured Colonel Grace, were entrenched behind breastworks atop the Confederate center in Colonel Robert C. Tyler's brigade of Brigadier General William B. Bate's division of Major General John C. Breckinridge's corps of Bragg's Army of Tennessee.[55] Late that afternoon Grant instructed Catholic, Irish-American Major General Phillip H. Sheridan to take four divisions and capture the Confederate rifle pits at the base of the ridge. The Federals took the position but could not hold it, because of the heavy fire of the Tenth Tennessee and other Southerners at the top. Without waiting for orders, the line officers and enlisted men of Sheridan's command charged up the ridge. Tyler's works were contested by Colonel Marshall F. Moore's "demi-brigade" (three regiments) of Union Brigadier General Richard Johnson's division.[56] When Tyler was seriously wounded, four of his six small regiments fell back to the summit, leaving only the Tenth and Thirtieth Tennessee regiments on the firing line.[57]

Colonel J. J. Turner, commanding the small unit of Tennesseans, repelled the charge of Irish-born Captain Patrick H. Keegan's Eleventh Michigan until the Federal Irishman was reinforced by Moore's other two regiments, the Nineteenth Illinois and the Sixty-Ninth Ohio. Turner withdrew his men from their works, using O'Neill's Irishmen as rear guards for the retirement.[58] Because of this deployment, the Sons of Erin had the distinction of being the last Southern troops to leave Bragg's center. Distinguishing themselves during the one-hour fight were O'Neill, Prendergast, and Captain Clarence C. Malone, a youthful Methodist, Irish-American from Mississippi. Missionary Ridge cost the Tenth Tennessee four killed, one wounded but not captured (Malone), ten wounded and captured, and seventeen captured but not wounded, for total losses of 32 out of 104, nearly one-third of those engaged.[59]

Grace was reactivated on the last day of 1863. Colonel Thomas Benton Smith replaced the wounded Tyler and commanded Tyler's brigade during all of 1864. For deployment purposes, Smith unofficially consolidated the remnant of the Irish regiment (sixty-nine effectives) with the even smaller Fourth Georgia Battalion Sharpshooters, using the combined unit as a rear guard.[60] As a result the Tennessee Irishmen were slightly engaged in six battles of the Atlanta campaign—Rocky Face Ridge, Resaca, New Hope Church, Decatur, Utoy Creek, and Jonesboro. O'Neill was seriously wounded at Resaca but recovered; Grace was mortally wounded at Jonesboro.[61] When Grace fell, Father Emmeran Bliemel, the German-born Benedictine who had replaced Father Browne as regimental chaplain, was decapitated by a Federal shell while administering the Last Rites to Grace, becoming the only Catholic chaplain on either side to be killed in action.[62]

Total losses (thirty-four) for the Tenth Tennessee in the Atlanta battles consisted of six killed (including Grace and Bliemel), twenty-one wounded and seven captured, nearly half of the sixty-nine men engaged.[63] The August 6, 1864, Battle of Utoy Creek was of note because it was the fourth and last skirmish of the war in which the Tennessee Irishmen inflicted several Union casualties while sustaining none themselves.

At the beginning of August, Benton Smith's brigade was to be found in Major General William B. Bate's division of Lieutenant General William J. Hardee's corps of the Army of Tennessee, commanded by Hood. Hood detached Bate from Hardee and temporarily assigned the division to Hood's old corps, commanded by Lieutenant General Stephen D. Lee. On August 4 Lee detached the six regiments of Smith's brigade, including the Tenth Tennessee, from Bate's division and posted the command of about 450 effectives slightly less than five miles southwest of Ezra Church along the east bank of the north tributary of Utoy Creek, where Major General John Schofield's Twenty-Third Corps of Major General William T. Sherman's army group was planning a crossing prior to attacking the Macon and Western Railroad.[64]

The Tennessee Irishmen and the other Southerners established a skirmish line on the east side of the creek and constructed breastworks one hundred yards east of the creek on a wooded hill.[65] Youthful General Benton Smith deployed his units from left to right, south to north: the Thirty-Seventh Georgia, the Fifteenth/Thirty-Seventh Tennessee Consolidated, the Twentieth Tennessee, the Thirtieth Tennessee, the Second Tennessee, and finally the Tenth Tennessee at the far right end of the line.[66]

Major General John Palmer, temporarily commanding Schofield's corps, ordered Brigadier General Jacob D. Cox of his Third Division to make a reconnaissance-in-force of the Confederate position. Cox gave the assignment to Brigadier General James W. Reilly of his First Brigade. To accomplish the task the Ohio Irish-American was given seven regiments: the Eighth U.S. Tennessee, the One-Hundred-

Twelfth Illinois, the One-Hundredth and One-Hundred-Fourth Ohio, and the Eleventh, Twelfth, and Sixteenth U.S. Kentucky.[67] Reilly established a skirmish line on the west bank of Utoy Creek with his command of about twelve hundred Northerners facing the smaller Southern force.

On the morning of Saturday, August 6, Smith set a trap for Reilly by sending an undersized detachment of pickets to hold down his skirmish line. This unit of about fifty men consisted of the Fourth Georgia Battalion Sharpshooters and half of the Tenth Tennessee. The Irish pickets were commanded by Captain John L. Prendergast.[68] When the One-Hundred-Fourth Ohio and the Eleventh U.S. Kentucky crossed the shallow stream, the Confederate skirmishers fired a few volleys before falling back to their main line. At eleven Reilly fell into Smith's trap when he instructed his lead two regiments to chase the Irishmen and the Georgians right up to the Confederate works.[69] The south end of the trenches, commanded by Smith himself, quickly dispersed the charging Ohioans. On the north end of the line (Union left, Confederate right) the Federal Kentuckians penetrated further than their Ohio comrades but were beaten back with heavy losses by the Thirtieth, Second, and Tenth Tennessee regiments, commanded by Grace.[70]

At 1 P.M., in response to Reilly's call for reinforcements, the One-Hundred-Twelfth Illinois, the One-Hundredth Ohio, and the Eighth U.S. Tennessee crossed the creek and advanced to within a few yards of the main Confederate position before being forced back, again with heavy losses. After the second Union wave had run its course, Bate reinforced Benton Smith's brigade with the Second and Fourth Kentucky regiments of the famed Orphan Brigade,[71] bringing the Southern numerical strength in that small sector up to about six hundred men, putting Tennessee and Kentucky troops on both sides of the engagement.

Smith commanded the troops on his left and rear, the Thirty-Seventh/Fourth Georgia, the Fifteenth/Thirty-Seventh Tennessee, and the Second/Fourth Kentucky. Grace, commanding Smith's right, consolidated his four regiments of about 250 effectives into one fighting unit—the Twentieth/Thirtieth/Second/Tenth Tennessee.[72] Reilly's third and last piecemeal assault, made shortly before three, was doomed from the start. His left flank was the Eighth U.S. Tennessee (223 effectives) commanded by Irish-American Captain J. W. Berry; his right flank was five companies of the One-Hundred-Fourth Ohio (less than 200 effectives) commanded by Irish-American Captain J. F. Riddle.[73] And so it was that about 400 highly exposed Federals charged some 600 well-entrenched Confederates. Riddle's weary Ohioans were almost immediately blasted away by Smith's Georgians, Tennesseans, and Kentuckians. Berry's East Tennesseans fought ferociously against Grace's Middle and West Tennesseans until Smith swung the two Irish companies of the Fourth Kentucky (D and H) over to support the right end of his line.[74]

When Berry wavered, Smith ordered a counterattack all along his front. After Reilly saw what was happening, he ordered a withdrawal of his assault force as well as his entire east-bank skirmish line back across the creek. On the south end of the field, Confederate Kentuckians chased after Federal Kentuckians, while on the north end of the field, a mounted Grace and his Irishmen and Tennesseans chased after Berry's Irishmen and Tennesseeans.[75] Smith wisely held his high ground and did not pursue Reilly's fleeing Federals.

The engagement at Utoy Creek ended around four o'clock, after three unsuccessful Union assaults and one successful Confederate counterassault. Benton Smith reported between "15 to 20 losses" out of about six hundred engaged; Reilly reported 306 losses out of about 900 engaged; and just like at Erin Hollow, O'Neill's Hill, and Reed's Bridge, Grace reported no losses for the Tenth Tennessee.[76] Following the action Prendergast and his Irish sharpshooters were given the honor of escorting the enemy prisoners to the rear. Three weeks later Grace was mortally wounded at Jonesboro. Twenty-two years later Episcopalian, Irish-American Captain Lewis R. Clark of the Sons of Erin expressed fond memories of a battle he remembered as "Utah Creek."[77]

In October of 1864 O'Neill, with the rank of lieutenant colonel, returned to active duty. His command numbered thirty-six officers and men, including himself.[78] During Hood's misguided invasion of Federally occupied Tennessee, the Sons of Erin participated in the battles of Franklin, Third Murfreesboro, and Nashville.[79] At Franklin, on November 30, the regiment suffered one killed, another wounded but not captured, still another captured but not wounded, and nine others both wounded and captured for total losses of twelve, precisely one-third of those engaged. Twenty of the remaining twenty-four were captured at Nashville on December 16, leaving only O'Neill, Clark, Seymour, and Catholic Irish-born Sergeant Bernard McCabe to be paroled with the Army of Tennessee at Greensboro, North Carolina, on May 1, 1865.[80]

During their four years of service the Tenth Tennessee had thirty men killed or mortally wounded, while twenty-six died in prison and another ten died of disease; ninety-one were disabled or seriously wounded. The Irishmen left an honorable record behind them; they consistently performed well as sharpshooters from a defensive deployment.

Several of these Middle Tennessee Irish Confederates survived into the twentieth century, including the following: Captain Charles H. Stockell of A Company, Lieutenant Colonel Samuel M. Thompson and Private John Connelly of B Company, Captain Clarence C. Malone of C Company, Private John Flemming of D Company, Captain Thomas Gibson and Sergeant Bernard McCabe of E Company, Corporal Michael Carney and Private Patrick M. Griffin of F Company, Second Lieutenant William W. Foote of G Company, First Lieutenant Lynch B. Donoho, Private William S. Lunn, Private John McElroy, and Private Daniel McCarthy, all of I company. Clarksville drummer-boy Danny McCarthy died at the age of ninety-two on January 17, 1940, exactly seventy-five years and forty-seven days after having been seriously wounded at the Battle of Franklin.[81]

The remains of German-born Lutheran Colonel Adolphus Heiman, Tennessee-born Presbyterian Colonel Randal W. McGavock, and Tennessee-born Catholic Colonel William Grace are interred at the Mount Olivet Episcopal Cemetery in Nashville. The final resting place of Irish-born Catholic Lieutenant Colonel John G. O'Neill, the last commanding officer of the Tenth Tennessee, is unknown.

NOTES

1. T. L. Connelly, *Army of the Heartland: Army of Tennessee 1861–1862* (Baton Rouge, 1965), p. 38; Stanley Horn, ed., *Tennesseeans in the Civil War: A Military History of Confederate and Union Units with Available Rosters of Personnel* (Knoxville, 1964–1965), vol. 1, p. 193.

2. Author's explanation of terms: The term "Irishmen" refers to those men who were immigrants or sons of immigrants. The term "Irish" is a description of those men whose parents or themselves came from the southern provinces (twenty-three counties) of Ireland; these men were mostly, but not exclusively, Catholics. The term "Scotch-Irish" is not used here in a strict historical sense, but merely serves as a general description of those men who ancestors came from the Ulster province of Ireland; these men were mostly, but not exclusively, Presbyterians and Methodists. The term "Anglo-Irish" is used to describe men of mixed Irish and English parentage; these men were mostly, but not exclusively, Episcopalians. Most of the Irishmen of the Tenth Tennessee were Catholics, but a significant minority of them were Protestants. The two Catholic chaplains of the regiment converted some of the "Anglo-Irish," like William Grace, to Catholicism, but had no such luck with the "Scotch-Irish" who were much more staunchly Protestant.

3. The flag is stored at the Tennessee State Museum in Nashville. The green coloring has faded to yellow. An original sketch is on file at the Buffalo Bill Museum in Cody, New York with Mr. Howard Michael Madaus.

4. There is a biography of McGavock, mostly about his pre-war activities, written by Herschel Gower and published in 1960 by McCowat Mercer Press at Jackson, Tennessee.

5. James D. Porter, *Confederate Military History: Tennessee* (Atlanta, 1899), p. 6.

6. "Troop Movements," Fort Donelson National Park map. Prepared in 1959 by Edwin C. Bearss.

7. Edwin C. Bearss, "The Fighting on February 13," Fort Donelson National Park Document No. 12, pp. 24–25.

8. James J. Hamilton, *The Battle of Fort Donelson* (Cranbury, New Jersey, 1968), p. 101.

9. Army Official Records (ORA) Series I, vol. 7, p. 203.

10 Jack Allen, and Herschel Gower, eds. "The Journals of Randal W. McGavock" (contained in *Pen and Sword*). Be it noted that the five main primary sources of the Tenth Tennessee are the journals of McGavock, the diary of Doyle, the narrative of Clark, the memoirs of Griffin, and the diary of Simpson.

11. The Diary of Jimmy Doyle 1861–1863, private collection of Margaret Bailey, Boston, Mass., p. 40.

12. Bearss Document No. 12, p. 24.

13. Wilbur F. Crummer, *With Grant at Fort Donelson, Shiloh, and Vicksburg* (Oak Park, Ill., 1915), p. 27.

14. Doyle diary, p. 39. (McGavock's personal colors are also stored at the Tennessee State Museum.)

15. Crummer, p. 28.

16. Doyle diary, pp. 39–40.

17. McGavock, p. 590; Porter, p. 21.

18. William Grace, Military Service Record; Doyle diary, p. 40.

19. McGavock, p. 590.

20 Tennessee Pension Records; Doyle diary, p. 40.

21. Hamilton, pp. 107–108.

22. Doyle diary, p. 40.

23. ORA series I, vol. 7, p. 204.

24. *Ibid.*, p. 367.

25. Oakwood Cemetery U.S. War Department Document No. 7.

26. Lewis R. Clark, "Tenth Tennessee Infantry." Published in *Military Annals of Tennessee: Confederate*. Edited by John B. Lindsley, M.D. (Nashville, 1886), pp. 284–285.

27. John G. Frank, "Adolphus Heiman: Architect and Soldier," *Tennessee Historical Magazine*. Annual 1946, vol. 5, p. 56.

28. Patrick M. Griffin, "The Famous Tenth Tennessee," *Confederate Veteran* magazine, December, 1905, vol. 13, pp. 554–555.

29. ORA, series I, vol. 24, Part 3, p. 737.

30 Edwin C. Bearss, *The Campaign for Vicksburg* (Dayton, 1986). vol. 2, pp. 492–493.

31. Edwin C. Bearss, "The Battle of Raymond," *Jackson* (Miss.) *Clarion*, February 12, 1958.

32. Bearss, *Campaign for Vicksburg*, vol. 2, p. 499.

33. Grant, U.S. "The Vicksburg Campaign," *Battles and Leaders of the Civil War (BL)* vol. 3, p. 503; Samuel Carter III. *The Final Fortress: The Campaign for Vicksburg* (New York, 1980 Reprint), p. 190.

34. Clark, p. 286.

35. *Ibid.*, Doyle diary, p. 50.

36. Doyle diary, pp. 50–51.

37. ORA series I, vol. 24, Part 3, p. 742.

38. *Ibid.*, p. 760.

39. *Ibid.*, p. 742; Doyle diary, p. 51.

40 Timothy Burgess, "Raymond Losses." Prepared for the author, 1991; Bearss, *Campaign for Vicksburg*, vol. 2, p. 515; Clark, p. 286.

41. ORA Series I, vol. 30, part 2, pp. 451–452.

42. *Ibid.*, part 1, p. 923; Doyle diary, p. 55.

43. Clark, p. 287.

44. Porter, p. 99.

45. ORA, Series I, vol. 30, part 2, p. 473, p. 481.

46. Clark, p. 287; Doyle diary, p. 57.

47. ORA, series I, vol. 30, part 2, pp. 457–458.

48. "Opposing Forces at Chickamauga," *BL*, vol. 3, pp. 672–676; Doyle diary, p. 59.

49. Clarence C. Malone Military Service Record; Clark, p. 287.

50 ORA, series I, vol. 30, part 1, p. 855, Part 2, p. 463; Archer Anderson, "Campaign and Battle of Chickamauga," *Southern Historical Society Papers (SHSP)*, September, 1881, vol. 9, p. 415.

51. ORA, Series I, vol. 30, Part 1, p. 809, p. 860, p. 867, part 2, p. 496; James Dinkins "The Battle of Chickamauga," *SHSP*, September, 1904, vol. 32, pp. 306–309.

52. Clark, p. 287.

53. Doyle diary, p. 62.

54. Clark, p. 290; Burgess, "Chickamauga Losses."

55. *Tennesseeans in the Civil War*, vol. 1, p. 195; Muster Roll Frame nos. 0022, 0024, 0026.

56. ORA, series I, vol. 31, part 2, p. 189, pp. 482–486, pp. 739–740;

James Lee McDonough, *Chattanooga: Death Grip on the Confederacy* (Knoxville, 1984), pp. 174–186; Henry M. Cist, *Army of the Cumberland* (New York, 1883), pp. 254–255.

57. Clark, p. 288.

58. *Ibid.*, ORA, series I, vol. 31, part 2, p. 743, pp. 480–481, p. 485; Porter, p. 116.

59. Clarence C. Malone military service record; Clark, p. 288; Burgess, "Missionary Ridge Losses."

60 Ed Porter Thompson, *History of the Orphan Brigade 1861–1865* (Louisville, 1898), pp. 244–246.

61. Clark, p. 288; Porter, p. 141.

62. Peter J. Meaney, O.S.B., "Valiant Chaplain of the Bloody Tenth," *Tennessee Historical Quarterly* (Spring 1982), vol. 41, p. 45.

63. Muster Roll Frame nos. 0032, 0034.

64. ORA, series I, vol. 38, part 3, pp. 676–682.

65. T. R. Roy, "General Hardee and the Military Operations Around Atlanta," *SHSP* (September-October 1880), vol. 8, pp. 359–366.

66. "Tennesseeans in Georgia," *Nashville Dispatch*, Monday, August 22, 1864.

67. Jacob B. Cox, *Atlanta* (New York, 1883), p. 190.

68. John L. Prendergast military service record.

69. ORA, series I, vol. 38, part 2, p. 705.

70 "Tennesseeans in Georgia."

71. ORA, series I, vol. 38, part 2, p. 689; Thompson, p. 264.

72. "Tennesseeans in Georgia."

73. ORA, series I, vol. 38, part 2, p. 690.

74. Muster Roll Frame No. 0034.

75. "Tennesseeans in Georgia"; Thompson, p. 264.

76. ORA, series I, vol. 38, part 2, p. 707, part 3, p. 765.

77. Clark, p. 289.

78. Muster Roll Frame No. 0190; *Tennesseeans in the Civil War*, vol. 1, p. 195.

79. Porter, pp. 154–168.

80 Muster Roll Frame nos. 0040, 0042.

81. May–June 1949, Letters of Barbara Ahern to Margaret Bailey. Margaret Bailey Collection, Boston.

PART II

WEST TENNESSEE IRISHMEN IN

CONFEDERATE SERVICE

THE MEMPHIS IRISH BRIGADE
  Second Tennessee Infantry Regiment (Walker's)
  Twenty-First Tennessee Infantry Regiment

ORGANIZED AS A MILITIA REGIMENT AT MEMPHIS on May 11, 1861, the Second Tennessee Infantry (Walker's) was mustered into regular Confederate service at Fort Pillow, Tennessee, on August 10. Oddly enough, the Irish Memphis unit should have been designated as the Third Tennessee, not the Second. On May 6, Colonel William B. Bate's Nashville-based regiment was registered with the state militia and then transferred to the army six days later. The staff of General Gideon Pillow, who commanded the Tennessee Home Guards, failed to take note of Bate's official registration date. Due to this clerical error there were two Second Tennessee Infantry regiments in Confederate service. The future General Bate had nine companies from the Nashville area, one from Memphis. Colonel Joseph Knox Walker, an Irish-American, who was the nephew and personal secretary of the late President James Knox Polk, was the commanding officer of the all-Memphis Second Tennessee. Like Presbyterian Randal W. McGavock, the colonel of the Tenth Tennessee, Walker was a Protestant (Episcopalian) with important connections to the Tennessee Catholic Diocese. In fact, Knox Walker had a pew reserved in his name at St. Patrick's Catholic Cathedral in Memphis. Also like McGavock of Nashville, Walker of Memphis was a lawyer-politician.[1]

Walker's Second Tennessee was one of the most urban outfits in the Confederacy. All officers and men were residents of the city of Memphis in Shelby County, mostly professionals and skilled laborers, very few farmers. Seven of the companies (B, C, F, G, H, I, K) consisted of Irishmen and Irish-Americans, while the other three companies (A, D, E) were formed from men of Old English stock. The religiously diverse Second Tennessee was more typically Southern Irish than the predominantly Catholic Tenth. Better than half the men were native-born high-church Protestants, especially Episcopalians and Methodists. Among the individual companies the heavily Irish-born Catholic F Company was a notable exception. This unit was composed of blacksmiths and carpenters who made up the Memphis Volunteer Fire Department. Company F was also the largest of the companies with four officers and seventy-three enlisted men, nearly all fire-fighters, nearly all parishioners of St. Patrick's. Colonel Walker's command was one of the smallest officially registered regiments on either side of the war with an original roster of only 541 officers and men, in size the equivalent of a battalion. In his haste to create an Irish brigade, Governor Isham G. Harris allowed the Memphis regiment to be formed from half-sized companies. This lack of normal man power would later create deployment problems for Knox Walker and his staff.[2]

The Memphis Irishmen of Colonel Walker were assigned to Major General Leonidas Polk's newly seized garrison at Columbus, Kentucky, on the Mississippi River, arriving at the Confederate "Gibraltar" on September 10, 1861. (General Polk, former bishop of the Louisiana Episcopal Diocese, was a distant relative of both President Polk and Colonel Walker, as well as a family friend of Colonel McGavock.) Strictly by accident, the Twenty-First Tennessee Infantry of Colonel Edward Pickett, Jr., reported on the same day from a separate transport. From that moment on the histories of the two Memphis regiments were locked together. The Twenty-First consisted of 744 officers and men, all from Memphis and Shelby County, farmers as well as tradesmen. About one-third of these men were Irishmen or Irish-Americans, mostly Presbyterians, Episcopalians, Methodists, Baptists, Congregationalists, and Unitarians. There was also a sprinkling of Irish-born Catholics, especially in D and E Companies. Pickett, a Methodist, had been the former editor of the *Memphis Daily Appeal*. Like Colonels Randal McGavock and Knox Walker, Colonel Ed Pickett was a Democratic Party politician from a prominent Irish-American Protestant family that had strong ties to Tennessee's emerging Irish-American Catholic community. The total number of effectives in both the Second and Twenty-First Tennessee regiments was 1,285, all from Shelby County, about 650 of whom were Irish-Americans, about one-third of whom were Catholics, about one-third of whom were the firemen of F Company, Second Tennessee, commanded by Irish-born Captain Samuel Vance, a member of the Order of Free-Masons.[3]

The Confederate guns at Columbus, nineteen miles south of the Federal Fort Defiance at Cairo, Illinois, protected the Upper Mississippi and the critical town of Memphis from the Union Army and Navy. General Albert Sidney Johnston commanded all Confederate forces in the West. Johnston at Bowling Green gave Polk at Columbus an entire army corps. In addition to the heavy artillery and some cavalry, the garrison was defended by twenty-five infantry regiments, including the Second and Twenty-First Tennessee, a total command of about 17,500 men. Directly across the river from Columbus on the west bank was Camp Johnston, Polk's observation post just below the three-farm river landing of Belmont, Missouri. Overly concerned about a Federal assault against his fortress on the Kentucky shore, General Polk kept only one of his regiments, the Thirteenth Arkansas, on the Missouri shore.[4]

Sidney Johnston's counterpart was Major General John C. Frémont, commanding all Union forces in the West. Frémont appointed Brigadier General U. S. Grant to head the District of Southeast Missouri. Frémont at St. Louis gave Grant at Cairo an entire army corps. Grant's command included twenty infantry regiments, sixteen of which were from Illinois, for a total of about 17,500 officers and men, almost exactly the same number as in Polk's command. General Frémont, who would soon be replaced by Major General Henry Halleck, also gave General Grant two objectives—one immediate, the other long term. The first goal was to clear the district from the cavalry raider activities of Confederate Missouri militia partisan M. Jeff Thompson, the former mayor of St. Joseph, known as the "Swamp Fox" of the South. The second and most important goal was to take Columbus back from General Polk.[5]

Faulty Union scouting reports led Grant at Cairo to believe that

Polk at Columbus was reinforcing Brigadier General Sterling Price, the former governor of Missouri and Grant's counterpart, by sending troops across the Mississippi from Columbus to Belmont. According to these reports, Polk's regulars, protected by Jeff Thompson's irregulars, were then heading west into the Missouri interior to link up with Price. None of it was true. Polk at Columbus was not reinforcing Price in Missouri and Thompson was not near Belmont. The aggressive U. S. Grant, however, figured that he could secure both his objectives at the same time. He would capture or destroy the pesky Thompson, soften up the defenses at Columbus by taking the Confederate camp at Belmont and eventually force the unaggressive Polk out of his garrison.[6]

On November 3 of 1861 "Uncle Sam" Grant sent a brigade under Colonel Richard J. Oglesby to do battle with Jeff Thompson's "Swamp Rats" in Missouri, while another brigade under Brigadier General Charles F. Smith was sent marching down from Paducah, Kentucky, with orders to probe the Southern defenses at Columbus. Meanwhile Grant himself would take five regiments on transports down the river, land on the western (Missouri) bank at Belmont and take Polk's observation post. The idea was for the three commands to join together. Oglesby's five regiments would drive Thompson further west and meet Grant's five regiments at Belmont. These ten regiments, protected by the Federal Navy, would then cross the river and join C. F. Smith's five regiments in an attack against Polk at Columbus. But Oglesby would not get to Belmont on time and Smith would not get to Columbus on time. On the morning of Thursday, November 7, Grant's 3,500 infantrymen landed at Hunter's Farm on the Missouri side of the Mississippi three miles above Belmont, as some 16,500 Confederates watched from the "Iron Banks" on the east bank.[7]

Colonel James E. Tappan of the Thirteenth Arkansas commanded Camp Johnston at Belmont. Along with his own regiment he had two companies of the First Mississippi Cavalry Battalion and the six guns of the Watson Artillery, a Catholic unit of New Orleans Creole gunners and Memphis Irish gunners. General Polk could see the Union Navy squadron protecting the troop transports in the river, but he had no information about enemy numbers. Cautiously the Louisiana general sent Brigadier General Gideon J. Pillow over to Belmont with four Tennessee regiments, including the Twenty-First, to reinforce Tappan. The coming battle would therefore pit the competent Grant and five Union regiments against the incompetent Pillow and five Confederate regiments.[8]

Grant's command was divided into two small brigades. The brigade from Cairo consisted of the Twenty-Seventh, Thirtieth, and Thirty-First Illinois Infantry regiments under Brigadier General John A. McClernand, the vain Southern Illinois politician. The men of the Twenty-Seventh were from the central part of the Prairie State; the men of the Thirtieth were from both the central and southern counties; and the men of the Thirty-First were exclusively from southern Illinois. The Irish-American colonel of the Thirty-First was Carbondale's John A. "Black Jack" Logan, a civilian soldier who would later command the Union Army of the Tennessee at the Battle of Atlanta. The brigade from Bird's Point, Missouri, a landing across the river and just below Cairo, consisted of the Twenty-Second Illinois Infantry and the Seventh Iowa Infantry under Irish-American Colonel Henry Dougherty. Like the Twenty-Seventh, the Twenty-Second was from the central counties of Illinois. The Seventh Iowa was a unit of farmers, mostly Germans and German Americans. Grant's order of battle was to march his five regiments inland west of the river with the intent of attacking Camp Johnston from the side and rear. McClernand's brigade led the way. Grant detached five of Dougherty's twenty companies (about seven hundred men) and kept them in reserve at Hunter's Farm with the boats. The Twenty-Second Illinois had to go into battle with only seven companies, the Seventh Iowa with only eight. All together General Grant advanced with about twenty-eight hundred men—about seventeen hundred of them with General McClernand, and other eleven hundred with Colonel Dougherty.[9]

General Pillow did not know what road the Federals were using, so he marched his five regiments a mile west of Camp Johnston and deployed a line in a series of cornfields, some of which were not even connected to the woods, an extremely poor choice for a defensive position. Pillow had about three thousand troops to defend against Grant's twenty-five hundred. From Confederate right to left (north to south) the Tennessean deployed the Twelfth Tennessee, the Thirteenth Arkansas, the Twenty-Second Tennessee, the partially Irish Twenty-First Tennessee, and the Thirteenth Tennessee. General Grant sent his Twenty-Seventh Illinois further south to penetrate the Confederate rear and deployed his other four regiments into an attack formation. Shortly after 10 A.M. the Federal skirmish line came off the road and charged General Pillow's line from west to east. The all-Irish Chicago Light Artillery Battery of Irish-born Captain Ezra Taylor, a devout Catholic, exchanged heavy fire with the New Orleans-Memphis Watson Battery of Maryland-born West Point graduate Lieutenant Colonel Daniel Beltzhoover of Mississippi, also a devout Catholic. The Protestant German farmers of Colonel Jacob G. Lauman attacked the totally exposed position held by the Protestant Memphis Irishmen of Colonel Ed Pickett. It was 10:15. The first of three bloody brawls between the Irishmen and the Germans was about to begin.[10]

Among the ranks of the Twenty-First Tennessee that day were Irishmen such as Privates Pat Burke, P. G. Burke, Pat Carroll, Denis Gleeson, Morris Moriarity, Phil Murphy, Roger O'Day, Dominick O'Donald, Owen Riley, and John Burke of E Company, a resident of Memphis who was twenty-five years old, five feet ten inches tall with dark complexion, dark hair, and brown eyes.

Pickett's men knelt in their cornfield and fired away at Lauman's men who were sheltered by trees some two hundred yards to the west. Even worse, the Tennesseans had only seven rounds of ammunition. In fact, after only twenty minutes of action, the entire Confederate command was running low on small-arms fire. In those early days of the war, a bayonet charge was considered a sound tactical device for an offensive movement. Pillow ordered one all along his front. To the right of the Irishmen of the Twenty-First Tennessee, the Twenty-Second Tennessee was being cut to pieces by a section of the predominantly Irish-Catholic Chicago Light Artillery Battery. To the left of the Twenty-First was the Thirteenth Tennessee, whose officers never got Pillow's message. Led by Irish-American Captain C. W. Frazier of I Company, the men of the Twenty-First raced through the cornfield with bayonets extended, unsupported on both flanks.[11]

A concentrated volley of musketry from the Iowa Germans rang out as Irish-American First Lieutenant Jesse Tate and about forty of the Memphis Irishmen went down. Irish-American Captain J. H. Healey of E Company and his men kept coming right up to the wooded position of the Union farmers and engaged them in a hand-to-hand combat. The assault of Healey's Irishmen stunned the Germans and they began to fall back further west into the woods in confusion. The Seventh Iowa was spared the necessity of full retreat by the Irishmen of the Chicago Battery who turned their guns away from the Twenty-Second Tennessee into the Twenty-First. Reinforced by elements of the Thirtieth Illinois, Colonel Lauman and his eight companies of Iowans counterassaulted a wooded position that had just been taken by Irish-American Captain J. D. Layton and the men of D Company, Twenty-First Tennessee. Layton and his Memphis men, reinforced by elements of the Twenty-Second Tennessee, put up a strong fight but without ammunition were forced back east out of the woods into the open cornfield. Colonel Pickett tried to rally the remnants of the Twenty-First and Twenty-Second regiments of Tennessee, but his horse was shot out from under him and the attempt failed. Better deployed and better supplied, the Illinoisans and Iowans had seized the moment. The Confederate situation worsened rapidly. By 10:45 General Pillow's line had collapsed.[12]

From high atop the Iron Banks at Columbus, General Polk could clearly see his Southerners running back east toward Camp Johnston with the Western Federals in hot pursuit. Very cautiously, the Confederate commander sent reinforcements across the river in the form of exactly one regiment. Polk's reinforcements would have to pay a heavy price for turning the tide of what seemed to be a sure Union victory. The regiment was the Second Tennessee, the Memphis Irishmen of Knox Walker. By eleven Pillow's troops were breaking rank and running north along the river bank in order to get out of Camp Johnston. The Twenty-Seventh Illinois continued to advance south while the other four Union regiments continued to advance east into the tent camp of the Thirteenth Arkansas. General Pillow placed Colonel Robert M. Russell of the Twelfth Tennessee in command of all the Confederates still in Camp Johnston, while Pillow rode north to look for the reinforcements coming off the transports. While the Federals were capturing the guns and some of the Irishmen of the Watson Battery and turning the artillery equipment over to the Irishmen of the Chicago Battery, General Pillow met Colonel Walker on the river bank just north of Camp Johnston, where the Irishmen of the Second Tennessee were posted in a wooded area.[13]

Among the ranks of the Second Tennessee that day were Irishmen such as Privates James Donohue, Philip Dougherty, George Finley, David Leahy, A. S. McCormick, Frank O'Brien, Michael Roach, William Shea, Patrick Sweeny, and M. T. Berry, a resident of Memphis who was twenty-four years old, five feet seven inches tall with fair complexion, light hair and gray eyes.

Pillow made an on-the-spot decision. Like Polk, the Tennessean was fond of creating makeshift brigades out of every two regiments for deployment purposes. Companies of the Twenty-First Tennessee were just then withdrawing north along the river road. Pillow sent for Pickett and ordered the newspaperman to report to Walker with the main body of his bloodied regiment. It was at this time that Pickett's Memphis Irishmen reinforced Walker's Memphis Irishmen on the wooded river bank. Pillow gave Walker command of the scratch brigade with Irish-American Lieutenant Colonel William B. Ross commanding the Second Tennessee. The only Irish Brigade for either side of the Western theatre of operations had been formed—accidentally and very temporarily. As Protestant Irish-American Confederates Walker, Pickett, and Ross were organizing a breakout from the woods, Protestant German-American Lauman took the battlefield initiative and led his command in pursuit of the retreating Southerners with hopes of capturing the lot of them. Jake Lauman's detachment consisted of his own Seventh Iowa up front, supported by some of Colonel Jack Logan's Southern Illinoisans coming up from Camp Johnston. The improvised Federal patrol marched up the river road to that point of the woods where Walker's brigade, supported by two of the companies of Lieutenant Colonel Alfred J. Vaughn's Thirteenth Tennessee, was concealed. It was shortly before 12 P.M. The second brawl between the Irishmen and the Germans was about to begin.[14]

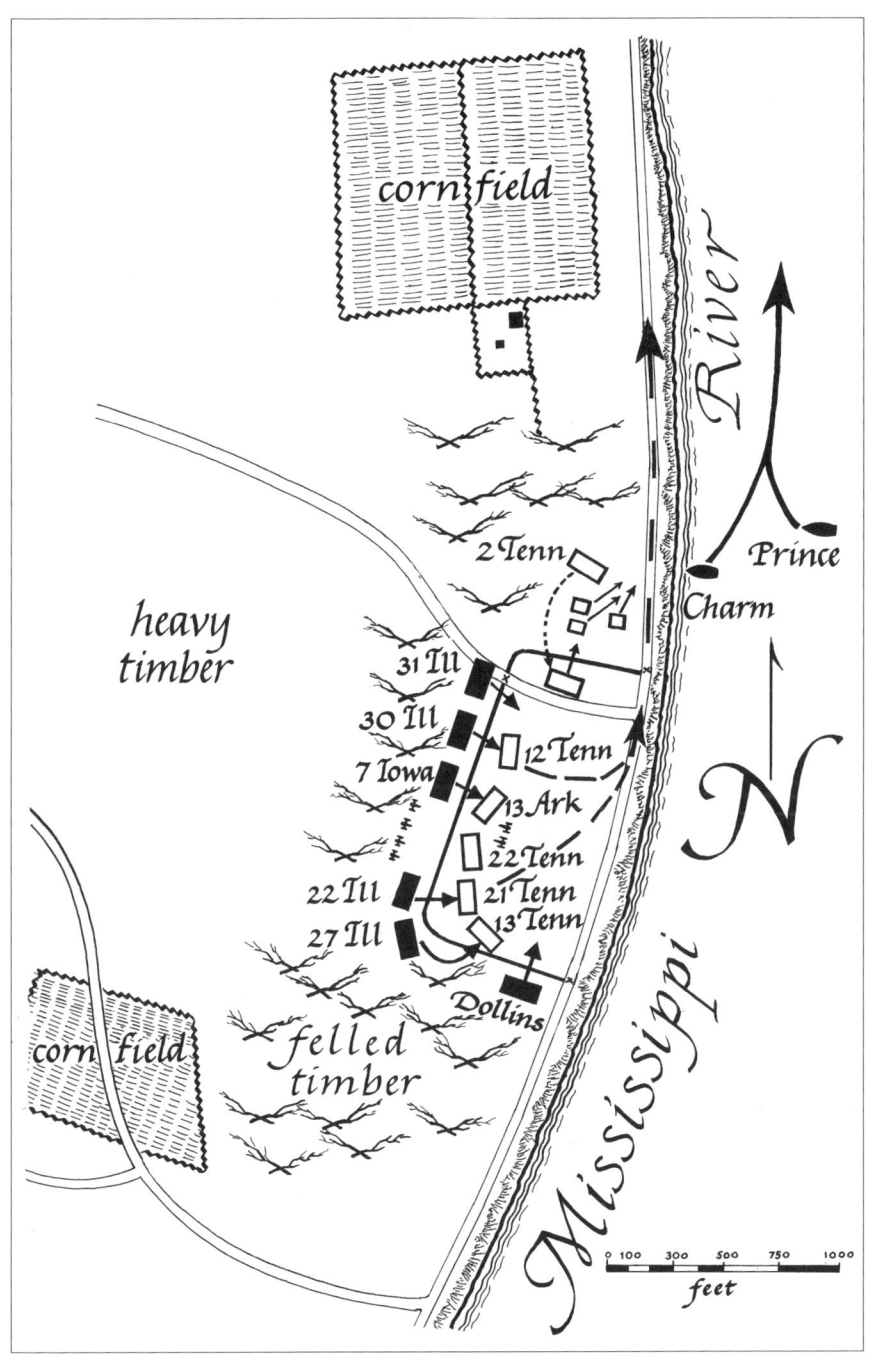

THE BATTLE OF BELMONT, MISSOURI

THURSDAY, NOVEMBER 7, 1861 — 11 A.M. POSITIONS

Colonel Walker assigned skirmish line duty to Captain Sam Vance of the Memphis Volunteer Fire Department. Vance, the high-degree Mason, divided F Company of the Second Tennessee into two platoons of about thirty foreign-born Irishmen each, one to be commanded by himself, the other by Second Lieutenant John Fitzgerald, an Irish-born Catholic. Vance needed every available Irishman, so he quickly recruited Sergeants Thomas Demmons and James Gilruth, both Irish-born Catholics from the quartermaster's staff, to his own command. Sam Vance's firemen quick-stepped south alongside of the river road toward the Illinoisans, while John Fitzgerald's firemen emerged from the woods into the side of the moving Seventh Iowa line. The Irishmen of Fitzgerald's platoon knelt and stood in a rotating double line formation while pouring several volleys into a section of the stunned Germans who had already been banged up from the morning encounter with Ed Pickett's Irishmen. During the skirmish line action of Vance's platoon, the captain was so pleased by Tom Demmons' capable performance that he immediately promoted his fellow foreign-born Irishman to the rank of brevet second lieutenant. Knox Walker deployed an assault wedge from northeast to southwest to be led by Bill Ross consisting of I Company, Second Tennessee, with some fifty men of the Twenty-First Tennessee. Unfortunately for the Confederates not all of the Memphis Irishmen proved to be heroes. To the unpleasant surprise of all, Irish-American Captain John L. Saffarans of I Company, with a bad case of nerves, hid in the woods and refused to advance. Later, Saffarans tried to stay out of harm's way by wading out into the river but his face was blown away by a Federal sharpshooter. Leading the men of I Company was First Lieutenant James "Jimmy" Walker, the nephew of the colonel. Ross' charge was extremely effective, causing many of the Iowans to throw down their weapons and run back down to Camp Johnston, stampeding some of the Illinoisans along the way. During this successful but brief assault of the Irish Brigade, youthful Jimmy Walker fought with great courage but was mortally wounded in full view of his uncle. Colonel Walker, with a numerical advantage of about a thousand men to five hundred, emptied his full force into the fight as Colonel Lauman rallied the remnant of his command.[15]

Once again the Chicago Irishmen saved the Iowa Germans from destruction at the hands of the Memphis Irishmen. Second in command of the Irish Chicago Light Artillery was German-born Captain Adolphus Schwartz. The Chicago German and some of his Irish gunners moved up two of the pieces from the Watson Battery that had been captured from the Memphis Irishmen of the Confederate Louisiana artillery unit. These guns poured a deadly storm of canister into the ranks of Ross' advancing columns. Some of the men of Walker's brigade panicked and fled back north to the woods along the river bank. Others held their ground and fought with desperation. German Federals Lauman and Schwartz, with their German infantrymen and Irish gunners, established a Union defensive line at the north end of Camp Johnston. English-born Captain J. Welby Armstrong of the Irish Brigade, commanding a small detachment, stabilized part of Walker's scattered force about two hundred yards south of the new Seventh Iowa position. Armstrong's improvised command consisted of about thirty of his own men from A Company, Second Tennessee, under Irish-American First Lieutenant L. D. Greenlaw and about twenty-five of the men from mixed companies of the Twenty-First Tennessee under Irish-American First Lieutenant James C. Cole. The heaviest fighting at the northern sector of the Belmont battlefield concluded around 12:30. The second brawl between the Irishmen and the Germans was indecisive. Walker's two Memphis regiments had, however, turned the tide of the battle. The Confederates would not yield any more ground. Three exhausted combat units licked their wounds and awaited further instructions—the Seventh Iowa, the Second Tennessee, and the Twenty-First Tennessee.[16]

While the second engagement between the Irishmen and the Germans raged, men from the main body of three Illinois regiments were back in Camp Johnston looting the Arkansas tents! While General Polk was sending more reinforcements over to General Pillow, General McClernand was making a pompous and premature victory speech. The celebration turned a small victorious army into a large rioting mob. General Grant had lost control over his own troops thanks to his glory-seeking Southern Illinois subordinate. As a result the Union commander ordered the camp to be burnt. He then ordered all five of his regiments back up toward Hunter's Farm and the awaiting boats.[17]

Gideon Pillow's latest reinforcements were two more regiments, which he promptly formed into another undersized brigade, consisting of the Eleventh Louisiana and the Fifteenth Tennessee, commanded by the aging Colonel Samuel F. Marks of the Louisiana regiment. Following these troops in another transport was Brigadier General Benjamin Franklin Cheatham and staff. Pillow informed Cheatham accurately that wounded Southerners in hospital tents had been consumed in the flames along with everything else. The Nashville general, a big fearsome-looking man, chased after Grant with a vengeance.[18]

Sam Marks' brigade caught up with elements of John McClernand's brigade while Frank Cheatham's division with the brigades of James Tappan, Robert Russell, and Knox Walker caught up with elements of Henry Dougherty's brigade. Black Jack Logan's regiment strongly resisted the advance of Marks' brigade until the Eleventh Louisiana and the Fifteenth Tennessee flanked the Thirty-First Illinois, forcing the southern Illinoisans to withdraw from their defensive line. Cheatham formed his own line of battle to the rear of the retreating Federal columns. This line was anchored by Tappan's men of the Thirteenth Arkansas, eager to avenge the death of their compatriots and the destruction of their camp. To the right and rear of the Arkansans were the men of Russell's brigade, the Thirteenth Tennessee, supported by the Twelfth Tennessee. To the left and rear of the Arkansans were the men of Walker's brigade, the Second Tennessee, supported by the remnants of the Twenty-First and Twenty-Second Tennessee. General Cheatham led the assault himself with Colonel Marks joining the offensive movement. It was eight Confederate regiments chasing after five Union regiments; that is, the brigades of Tappan, Russell, Walker, and Marks against the brigades of McClernand and Dougherty. Wrongly believing that Southerners had been burned alive intentionally, the Confederates attacked the outnumbered and demoralized Federals with great ferocity. In the middle of the wooded field, Tappan collided with the Thirtieth Illinois of Colonel Philip B. Fourke. On the east end of the field Russell collided with some of the companies of the Twenty-Second and Thirty-First Illinois. On the west end of the field Walker collided with the Seventh Iowa and other companies of the Twenty-Second Illinois, commanded by Irish-American Lieutenant Colonel Harrison E. Hart. It was 1:30. The bloody third and last brawl between the Irishmen and the Germans was about to begin.[19]

Knox Walker advanced at a run with a skirmish line detachment that consisted of Welby Armstrong and the men of A and G companies, Second Tennessee, along with about forty of the Memphis Irishmen of the Watson Battery serving as infantry. The Englishman was killed and several of the Irish-Americans of G Company were wounded by an artillery barrage from Irish-born First Lieutenant Patrick White's section of the Irish Chicago Battery. When John Fitzgerald and the Irish-born firemen of F Company moved up to replace the fallen Armstrong and his command, the advance of the Irish Brigade surged ahead with Bill Ross' men coming out of the woods to the left (west) and with Ed Pickett's men emerging from the woods on the right (east). Ross' detachment consisted of the seven companies of the Second Tennessee that were not with Armstrong or Fitzgerald. Pickett's detachment consisted of the remaining men of his own Twenty-First Tennessee plus some of the men of Colonel Thomas J. Freeman's Twenty-Second Tennessee. Jake Lauman's horse was shot out from under him. Although the German commander was in considerable pain from the fall, he refused to be taken to the rear. The remnant of the Seventh Iowa, supported by the last two companies of Harrison Hart's Twenty-Second Illinois, backed off slowly with Tennesseans, Iowans, and Illinoisans suffering casualties every step of the way. During this action two of the men of J. D. Greenlaw's A Company of Bill Ross' Second Tennessee were permanently disabled. They were Privates Hugh B. Baxter and Frank Beamish.[20]

Beamish was a twenty-nine-year-old laborer from Madison, Arkansas, who had been born in Monroe County, New York. Five feet nine inches tall with light complexion, blue eyes, and light hair, Beamish was inflicted with a compound fracture of the tibia on his right leg caused by a Federal gunshot. He became disabled for life when the same leg was wounded again at Shiloh. Baxter was a twenty-four-year-old farmer from Crockett Mills, Tennessee, who had been born in County Deery, Ireland, emigrating to America in 1857. Baxter's foot was shattered by a fragment from a Federal shell, resulting in permanent lameness. Forty-six years later the Irishman applied for a pension from the state of Tennessee. The examining doctor reported that eighty-year-old Hugh Baxter was greatly disabled and had a crooked leg that had been caused by a fracture. Oddly enough the disability was not considered a direct result of the Belmont wound. The pension was granted in any case.[21]

As the third brawl between the Irishmen and the Germans reached a bloody climax, the focus of attention was concentrated on the battle flag of the Seventh Iowa. Company K of the Second Tennessee, led by Catholic Irish-born Sergeant Dennis Lynch and by Episcopalian Private David Vollmer, a native Tennessean of Old English stock, savagely fell upon the color-guard of the German farmers. While Lynch used his musket as a club, Vollmer plunged his bayonet into the Iowa color-bearer, then seized the banner and held it high to the shouts of the Irish Brigade. On the reverse side of the flag was the stars and stripes covered in blood. Within a minute, however, Lynch and Vollmer were both killed by multiple musketry and the German Union colors were recaptured. By this time the decimated Seventh Iowa had few officers left standing. Some of the men of the Twenty-Second Illinois formed a rear guard for the Iowa Germans as the Federals continued their withdrawal toward Hunter's Farm. Colonels Walker, Pickett, and Ross no longer had any intact companies for an effective pursuit. Small bands of Tennesseans, Illinoisans, and Iowans skirmished here and there. Walker's and Lauman's commands had, in reality, destroyed each other with both sides mixing in a little bit of military skill and remarkable amounts of raw courage. The Seventh Iowa would be badly bloodied again at Fort Donelson before disappearing from history. The Second and Twenty-First Tennessee would never again be viable combat units.[22]

By 2:30 Cheatham had drained most of the fight out of the Federals who continued to straggle back up to the landing. At this time Leonidas Polk himself landed on the Missouri shore with two more infantry units from Columbus, giving Pillow the opportunity to create still another scratch brigade. The fifth and last Confederate brigade, commanded by Colonel Preston Smith, consisted of the First Mississippi Infantry battalion and Smith's own One-Hundred-Fifty-Fourth Senior Tennessee Infantry regiment, the latter being another Memphis unit with two companies of Irishmen. Preston Smith's brigade was, however, never heavily engaged. Of the twelve Confederate units at Belmont, four had a significant representation of Memphis Irishmen—the Second Tennessee, the Twenty-First Tennessee, the One-Hundred-Fifty-Fourth Senior Tennessee, and the Watson Battery. Late in the afternoon the remnant of the five Union regiments escaped to the safety of their transports, and along with the Navy squadron, sailed back up to Cairo with the aroused Confederates firing at them from both river banks. In spite of the defeat, President Abraham Lincoln was pleased by the aggressiveness of fellow-Illinoisan U. S. Grant.[23]

Between 10:15 and 10:45 A.M. the Seventh Iowa, reinforced by the Thirtieth Illinois, defeated the Twenty-First Tennessee reinforced by the Twenty-Second Tennessee. At noon the Memphis Irish Brigade was formed. Between 12:15 and 12:45 P.M. the Seventh Iowa, reinforced by the Thirty-First Illinois, fought the Second Tennessee and the Twenty-First Tennessee, reinforced by the Thirteenth Tennessee, to a draw. Between 1:30 and 2:15 the Second Tennessee and the Twenty-First Tennessee, reinforced by the Twenty-Second Tennessee, defeated the Seventh Iowa reinforced by the Twenty-Second Illinois. Colonel Pickett performed well in the morning; Colonels Walker and Ross performed well in the afternoon. The final margin of victory for the Irishmen over the Germans was very narrow. The exhausted Tennesseans allowed the exhausted Iowans to withdraw from the field. After 2:30 Walker's temporary Irish brigade was no longer deployed, as all of the Southerners left on the field were placed under the direct command of General Polk.[24]

The Federals had 606 men killed, wounded, missing or captured out of about 2,500 engaged, representing total losses of twenty-four percent. The Seventh Iowa alone had 31 killed, 77 wounded, and 114 missing or captured for a total of 222 losses out of the 512 men engaged; that is, forty-three percent, the Union Army's worst regimental totals during the war's first year. Thirty-seven percent of all Federal losses at Belmont came from the one German farmer regiment, causing a storm of protest to follow from the citizens of Iowa. The Confederates had 671 men killed, wounded, missing, or captured out of about 5,200 engaged, representing total losses of thirteen percent. The Twenty-First Tennessee had 13 killed, 62 wounded, and 5 missing or captured for total losses of 80 out of 744, eleven percent. The Second Tennessee had 18 killed, 63 wounded, and 33 missing or captured for total losses of 114 out of 541, twenty-one percent. Taken together the two regiments of Walker's brigade suffered 194 losses out of 1285 men or sixteen percent of those engaged. The Memphis Irish Brigade therefore sustained twenty-nine percent of all Confederate losses. Including casualties from the Irishmen of the Watson Battery, Memphis Irish units suffered nearly one-third of all Southern losses at Belmont. Remarkably Walker's two regiments and Lauman's regiment had exactly the same number of men killed, 31. In the end, the Confederate Irishmen won out against the Federal Germans because of superior numbers. It was like the rest of the war in reverse.[25]

Following the Battle of Belmont there was considerable dissatisfaction among the men of both the Second and Twenty-First Tennessee Infantry regiments. Desertions further depleted the ranks. In December of 1861 Colonel Pickett reported that 447 officers and men were present for duty, while Colonel Walker reported a total of 357. On March 9, 1862, Pickett's command was assigned to garrison duty at the Confederate recruitment camp at Union City, Tennessee. On the last day of that month a detachment of Union cavalry and infantry raided the camp. The attack caught the Memphis Tennesseans completely by surprise and they fled in disorder without firing a shot, abandoning their tents which were then confiscated by the enemy. Ed Pickett was blamed by General P. G. T. Beauregard and forced to resign, his heroics at Belmont seemingly forgotten. A small remnant of the Twenty-First awaited future reassignment.[26]

Knox Walker's Second Tennessee was placed in Brigadier General Bushrod R. Johnson's brigade of Cheatham's division of Polk's corps of Sidney Johnston's army. On April 6, 1862—on the morning of the first day of the Battle of Shiloh—half of the Memphis Irishmen were withheld in a separate sector while the other half was deployed as a small support unit behind the Fifteenth Tennessee Infantry in front of a heavily fortified Ohio-based Union position. The Tennesseans suffered severe losses from an enemy artillery barrage. When the Second was ordered to advance with the Fifteenth, the Irishmen twice refused, while many of them ran to the rear. Walker resigned shortly after the Shiloh incident and died in 1864. A small remnant of his regiment awaited future reassignment.[27]

During June of 1862 the Irishmen of the Memphis Volunteer Fire Department transferred from F Company of the Second Tennessee (Walker's) to E Company of the Second Tennessee (Bate's), the lone Memphis company of that Nashville regiment, which was then commanded by Irish-American Colonel William D. Robinson. At the Battle of Utoy Creek, August 6, 1864, the Memphis fire-fighters fought side-by-side with the Middle Tennessee Irishmen of the Tenth. In July of 1862 the last of Walker's men and the last of Pickett's men were consolidated into a single regiment identified as the Fifth Confederate Infantry under Irish-American Colonel James A. Smith, formerly of Walker's command. In reality it was a small battalion of 343 officers and men, about half of whom were of Irish ancestry. The Fifth Confederate was placed in Brigadier General Lucius Polk's brigade of Cheatham's division. Generals Cheatham and L. Polk (nephew of General Leonidas Polk) both praised the efforts of Smith and his men at the Battles of Perryville and First Murfreesboro. Later the Fifth Confederate was consolidated with the Third Confederate (another unit consisting originally of two Tennessee regiments) and assigned to the division of Irish-born Major General Patrick R. Cleburne. Of the 1,285 men who were with Colonels Walker and Pickett at Belmont, ten were still in the Army of Tennessee at the time of surrender. When the Tennessee volume of *Confederate Military History* was published in 1899, there was a biographical section in the back of the book. Not a single soldier of the Second Tennessee (Walker's), the Twenty-First Tennessee, or the Fifth Confederate was mentioned. These regiments, along with the Seventh Iowa, remain some of the most obscure units in American military history.[28]

The Battle of Belmont, Missouri
Thursday, November 7, 1861
Command Structure After 12:00 P.M.

Confederate Forces
(105 companies, about 5,200 effectives)
Major General Leonidas Polk
Brigadier General Gideon J. Pillow
Brigadier General Benjamin Franklin Cheatham

Tappan's Brigade
Colonel James C. Tappan

13th Arkansas Inf. Reg.	Col. James C. Tappan
1st Mississippi Cav. Batt. (2 Co.)	Lt. Col. John H. Miller
Watson Battery (6 guns)	Lt. Col. Daniel Beltzhoover

Russell's Brigade
Colonel Robert M. Russell

12th Tennessee Inf. Reg.	Lt. Col. Tyree H. Bell
13th Tennessee Inf. Reg.	Col. John V. Wright
22nd Tennessee Inf. Reg.	Col. Thomas J. Freeman

Walker's Brigade (Memphis Irish Brigade)
Colonel J. Knox Walker

2nd Tennessee Inf. Reg.	Lt. Col. William B. Ross
21st Tennessee Inf. Reg.	Col. Edward Pickett Jr.

(gunners of the Watson Battery fighting as infantry)

Marks' Brigade
Colonel Samuel F. Marks

11th Louisiana Inf. Reg.	Lt. Col. Robert H. Barrow
15th Tennessee Inf. Reg.	Lt. Col. Robert C. Tyler

SMITH'S BRIGADE
Colonel Preston Smith
154th Senior Tennessee
    Infantry Regiment   Lt. Col. Marcus J. Wright

1ST MISSISSIPPI INF. BATT.
  (5 companies)   Lt. Col. Andrew K. Blythe
White's Batt. Tenn. Cav.
  (2 companies)   Capt. Josiah White

UNION FORCES
(52 companies, about 2,500 effectives)
Brigadier General U. S. Grant
Brigadier General John A. McClernand
Colonel Henry Dougherty

FIRST BRIGADE
Brigadier General John A. McClernand
  27th Illinois Inf. Reg.   Col. Napoleon B. Buford
  30th Illinois Inf. Reg.   Col. Philip B. Fourke
  31st Illinois Inf. Reg.   Col. John A. Logan
  Dollins Batt. Illinois Cavalry
  (2 companies)   Capt. James J. Dollins

SECOND BRIGADE
Colonel Henry Dougherty
  22nd Illinois Inf. Reg.
  (7 companies)   Lt. Col. Harrison E. Hart
  7th Iowa Inf. Reg.
  (8 companies)   Col. Jacob G. Lauman
  Chicago Light Artillery
  Battery (6 guns)   Capt. Ezra Taylor
  Delano's Batt. Illinois Cav.
  (2 companies)   First Lt. James K. Catlin

NOTES

1. Sally Walker Boone, "After the Battle of Belmont," Tennessee State Library and Archives (TSLA) Manuscript No. 313, pp. 1–2; James A. Smith, "Second Tennessee Infantry," pp. 173–174 John B. Lindsley, ed., *The Military Annals of Tennessee: Confederate* (Nashville, 1886).

2. Ed Gleeson, *Rebel Sons of Erin* (Indianapolis, 1993), p. 294; Stanley Horn, ed., *Tennesseeans in the Civil War*. Civil War Centennial Commission, (Nashville, 1965), vol. 1, "Second Tennessee Infantry," p. 174, p. 176; Elbert L. Watson, "James Walker of Columbia," *Tennessee Historical Quarterly* (*THQ*), vol. 23 (March 1964), pp. 24–37.

3. John Fitzgerald, Military Service Record (MSR), National Archives and Records Administration (NARA), Confederate Record Group (RG) No. 109; Michael T. Michell, *Memphis During the War Between the States: Personalities and Profiles* (Memphis, 1895), p. 34; George C. Porter, "Tennessee Confederate Regiments: The Twenty-First," Civil War Collection, Confederate Clippings No. 52, TSLA.

4. Thomas L. Connelly, *Army of the Heartland: Army of Tennessee* (Baton Rouge, 1988), p. 52; Patricia L. Faust, ed., *Historical Times Illustrated: Encyclopedia of the Civil War* (New York, 1986), p. 54.

5. Connelly, pp. 103–104; F. V. Greene, *The Mississippi* (New York, 1883), pp. 4–6.

6. Mark M. Boatner III, ed., *Civil War Dictionary* (New York, 1959), pp. 57–58; Stanley Horn, *Army of Tennessee* (Indianapolis, 1941), p. 63.

7. E. B. Long, ed., *Civil War Almanac, Day By Day: 1861–1865* (New York, 1971), p. 136; *St. Louis Sunday Republican*, Nov. 10, 1861; *Weekly Missouri* (St. Louis) *Democrat*, Nov. 13, 1861.

8. Robert W. Barnwell, "The Battle of Belmont," *Confederate Veteran* magazine (*CV*), vol. 39, pp. 370–371; William M. Polk, "General Polk and the Battle of Belmont," *Battles and Leaders of the Civil War* (*BL*), vol. 1, p. 348.

9. Henry I. Kurtz, "The Battle of Belmont," *Civil War Times Illustrated* (*CWTI*), vol. 3 (June 1963), p. 19; John Y. Simon, "Grant at Belmont," *Military Affairs Magazine* (*MAM*), vol. 45 (Dec. 1981), pp. 164–165.

10. *Memphis Daily Appeal*, Nov. 14, 1861; James D. Porter, *Confederate Military History: Tennessee* (*CMH*) (Atlanta, 1899), p. 11; Official Records of the Armies (ORA), series I, vol. 3, p. 360; Adolphus Schwartz, "Report of the Battle of Belmont," *Chicago Historical Society* (*CHS*).

11. Tyree H. Bell, "Report of the Battle of Belmont." Southern Illinois University Library (SIU), Carbondale; John Seaton, "The Battle of Belmont," *CHS*; Don Singleton, "The Battle of Belmont," *CV*, vol. 23, pp. 506–507.

12. J. H. Healey, J. D. Layton, E. Pickett, J. Tate: MSR, TSLA; *Nashville Banner*, Nov, 12, 1861; Henry I. Smith, *History of the Seventh Iowa Veteran Volunteer Infantry* (Mason City, Ia., 1903), p. 252; Marcus M. Wright, "The Battle of Belmont," *Southern Historical Society Papers* (*SHSP*), vol. 16, p. 73.

13. Horn, *Army of Tennessee*, p. 64; George H. Hubbard, "In the Battle of Belmont, Mo.," *CV*, vol. 30, p. 459; Nathaniel E. Hughes, Jr., *The Battle of Belmont: Grant Strikes South* (Chapel Hill, 1991), p. 118.

14. C. C. Carpenter, and G. W. Crossley, "Seventh Iowa Volunteers in the Civil War Gave Valiant Service," *Annals of Iowa* (*AI*), vol. 34 (1957), pp. 101–102; Kurtz, "Belmont," *CWTI*, vol. 30, p. 20; ORA, vol. 3, p. 334.

15. Boone, "After Belmont," TSLA, pp. 3–4; J. Fitzgerald, M. B. Ross, J. L. Saffarans, James Walker: MSR, TSLA; Hughes, *Belmont*, p. 123; Smith, *Seventh Iowa*, p. 252; William G. Stevenson, *Thirteen Months in the Rebel Army* (New York, 1862), p. 40, p. 70.

16. J. W. Armstrong, MSR, NARA, RG109; Arthur W. Bergeron, Jr., *Guide to Louisiana Confederate Military Units 1861–1865* (Baton Rouge, 1989), pp. 36–37; Dimitry, John. *Louisiana CMH*, pp. 162–163; *Memphis Daily Appeal*, Nov. 12, 1861; Schwartz, "Belmont," *CHS*.

17. U. S. Grant, *Personal Memoirs* (New York, 1886), vol. 1, p. 274; Horn, *Army of Tennessee*, p. 65; John A. McClernand, "Report of the Battle of Belmont," CHS; Seaton, "Belmont," *CHS*.

18. Bergeron, *Louisiana Units*, p. 99; Timothy D. Johnson, "Benjamin Franklin Cheatham at Belmont," *Missouri Historical Review* (*MHR*), vol. 81 (1986–87), pp. 159–172; Wright, "Belmont," *SHSP*, vol. 16, p. 72.

19. Bell, "Belmont," SIU; Hughes, *Belmont*, p. 143; *New Orleans Daily Crescent*, Nov. 13, 1861; ORA, vol. 3, p. 361; James D. Porter, *Tennessee*, p. 12.

20. J. W. Armstrong, MSR, NARA, RG109; W. W. Carnes, "The Battle of Belmont." *CV*, vol. 39, p. 369; *Chicago Tribune*, Nov. 11, 1861; J. Fitzgerald: MSR, TSLA; Hubbard, "Belmont," *CV*, vol. 30, p. 459.

21. H. B. Baxter, F. Beamish: MSR, TSLA; H. B. Baxter Pension File No. 9743, TSLA.

22. Bell, "Belmont," SIU; Boone, "After Belmont," TSLA, pp. 5–6; Hughes, *Belmont*, pp. 143–144, p. 155; *Memphis Daily Appeal*, Nov. 12, 1861; *Nashville Banner*, Nov. 13, 1861; *Nashville Daily Gazette*, Nov. 10, 1861; Smith, *Seventh Iowa*, p. 252.

23. Kurtz, "Belmont," *CWTI*, vol. 3, p. 21; *New Orleans Daily Crescent*, Nov. 13, 1861; W. B. Polk, "Belmont," *BL*, vol. 1, p. 351; Charles Quintard, "B. F. Cheatham, CSA." *SHSP*, vol. 16, p. 351; *St. Louis Sunday Republican*, Nov. 10, 1861.

24. *Memphis Daily Appeal*, Nov. 9, Nov. 12, Nov. 21, 1861; ORA, vol. 3, p. 308; James D. Porter, *Tennessee*, p. 13.

25. *Daily Missouri* (St. Louis) *Republican*, Nov. 15, 1861; *Daily Nashville Patriot*, Nov. 15, 1861; Hughes, *Belmont*, pp. 184–185; Long, *Almanac*, p. 136; *Memphis Daily Appeal*, Nov. 17, 1861; W. B. Polk, "Belmont," *BL*, vol. 1, p. 353, pp. 355–356; *St. Louis Weekly Democrat*, Nov. 19, 1861.

26. E. Pickett, J. K. Walker: MSR, TSLA; E. Pickett, J. K. Walker: Regimental Muster Rolls, NARA, RG109; George C. Porter, "The Twenty-First," Confederate Clippings Collection No. 52, TSLA; *Tennesseeans in the Civil War* (*TCW*), vol. 1, p. 220.

27. Wiley Sword, *Shiloh: Bloody April* (Dayton, 1988), p. 206; *TCW*, vol. 1, p. 175.

28. Gleeson, *Rebel Sons*, p. 299; Fifth Confederate Infantry Regimental Muster Rolls, NARA, RG109; *TCW*, vol. 1, pp. 175–176.

PART III

EAST TENNESSEE IRISHMEN IN

CONFEDERATE SERVICE

THE IRISH MOUNTAINEERS
  B Company, Third Confederate Battalion
  Engineer Corps
  Department of East Tennessee

IN THE EARLY FALL OF 1861 A MEETING TOOK PLACE somewhere in the Irish settlement of Rogersville, Hawkins County, amidst the mountains of East Tennessee. Present were as many as thirty-four men, all construction workers and laborers, all Irish-born Catholics, a number of whom came from County Clare. At this gathering it was determined that the small but highly visible Irish community of Hawkins County would join the Confederate Army as a unit of engineers. Since a substantial majority of East Tennessee's Irishmen were pro-Union, the Rogersville decision remains somewhat of a mystery. The leader of the group was William Thomas Houck, a thirty-five-year-old stone mason from County Clare. Two of his neighbors, John Condon, age thirty-four, and Thomas Francis Cooley, age thirty-eight, also stone masons from County Clare, had similar backgrounds. All three Irishmen emigrated to America in the 1840s, settled in Virginia, and raised large families. Because of their backgrounds, these three Irish East Tennesseans may well have still considered themselves Virginians, loyal to the South. This might explain their service with the Confederacy. But it is only a guess.[1]

In any case W. T. Houck was elected "captain" of the "company." In late October the thirty-four Irishmen reported to Confederate authorities in Knoxville where they were mustered at first into state militia service and then into regular Confederate service. Apparently at that time no other Hawkins County engineering unit could be found to detach Houck's command to. On November 11, 1861, the Richmond War Department officially registered the Irish mountaineers as "Houck's Independent Company, East Tennessee Engineers." The "captain" was commissioned as a second lieutenant, the only officer of the undersized company which was, in fact, a mere platoon. Houck appointed his County Clare stone mason friends as his subordinates. Condon became the only sergeant of the unit; Cooley became the only corporal. The independent Irish company was stationed in Hawkins County for the next six months, their duties unknown. The Irishmen probably spent considerable time with their families at home. There were no resignations or desertions reported in the unit.[2]

By the spring of 1862 there was an independent company of Confederate engineers operating in the Monroe and Washington Counties of East Tennessee, consisting of two officers and seventy-five enlisted men, a mix of skilled laborers from the western counties of Virginia and the eastern counties of Tennessee. The commanding officer was First Lieutenant Lawrence A. McCauley, an Irish-American Virginian. He was assisted by Second Lieutenant George Margrave, an Irish-American East Tennessean. A sprinkling of Irish names appeared on the muster rolls. In April of 1862 McCauley and Houck were both ordered to Knoxville with their commands. On May 12 the two companies were formed into an extremely obscure unit known as the "Third Confederate Battalion, Engineer Corps, Department of East Tennessee." McCauley's men became A Company; Houck's Irishmen became B Company. In reality the unit of three officers and ninety-eight enlisted men was a company, not a battalion, a reality that was indicated by the ranking of the officers. McCauley was promoted to captain, the commanding officer of the unit. Margrave was promoted to first lieutenant, commanding A Company. Houck commanded B Company with the same rank of second lieutenant.[3]

Also in 1862 the Department of East Tennessee was temporarily called the Army of Kentucky under Major General Edmund Kirby Smith. McCauley's engineers were, however, on special assignment to General Braxton Bragg, commanding the Army of the Mississippi. During that summer Bragg made plans to invade the Federal state of Kentucky using his command and Kirby Smith's command, a campaign that resulted in the Battle of Perryville on October 8. By early September both Southern armies had marched out of Tennessee into Kentucky. The men of the Third Confederate Battalion, Engineers, were down in East Tennessee repairing bridges along Bragg's supply routes. Captain McCauley joined Lieutenant Margrave and assigned A Company to a bridge at Rogers Gap, a few miles south and west of Cumberland Gap, where the boundaries of Kentucky, Tennessee, and Virginia meet. Lieutenant Houck and the Irishmen of B Company were sent back a few miles further south and west of Rogers Gap to a smaller bridge near Big Creek Gap. There were two work sites at Big Creek, one commanded by Houck, the other by Sergeant John Condon.[4]

On Wednesday, September 10, 1862, with no warning and with no offer to surrender, Condon's detachment of eleven men was fired on by a small band of pro-Union East Tennessee partisans. The Irish Confederate engineers apparently had some arms and some horses. Sergeant Condon put together an impromptu defense that has never been described in any detail. It is certain, however, that he was wounded and captured. Three of his men were also captured. Corporal T. F. Cooley and six others escaped on horseback. The corporal later credited Condon with saving his life. Houck's detachment was also attacked by other elements of the same party of bushwhackers. The second lieutenant and twenty of his Irishmen escaped. Two of Houck's men were captured, one of whom was wounded. The brief and one-sided skirmish at Big Creek Gap left B Company with six men captured out of thirty-four, two of whom were also wounded including John Condon who permanently lost the use of an arm. The Union irregulars delivered the six Irishmen to Federal authorities for a bounty. The prisoners were then shipped off to Camp Chase in Columbus, Ohio, where they remained for ten long months. Records indicate that all six survived. Two months later Lieutenant Houck reported that four of his Irishmen, including Corporal Cooley, had resigned from the army for personal reasons and had returned home. Houck noted that all four were family men. With ten losses Houck's command was reduced to one officer and twenty-three men. As a result of this, Captain McCauley abolished B Company and consolidated his command into a single unit with George Margrave continuing to serve as first lieutenant and with William Houck continuing to serve as second lieutenant. In December of 1862 McCauley's company was reported to be in Knoxville. The war department continued to refer to the unit as the Third Confederate Battalion, Engineer Corps.[5]

In February 1863 Thomas F. Cooley sent a replacement for himself from Rogersville to Knoxville. The replacement was James L. Cooley, age twenty, the oldest son. The father remained at home with the rest of his large family, while the son served the Confederacy. In the spring Lawrence McCauley was reassigned to his native Virginia where he raised another engineering company. George Margrave took command of McCauley's company with William Houck as his only commissioned subordinate. In spite of the official battalion designation neither lieutenant appears to have ever been promoted. In the fall of 1863 Margrave's independent company of engineers, some seventy-five men including Private Cooley, were detached to the Confederate camp at Charleston, Tennessee, for the duration of the conflict, their duties again unknown. After the war the Irish veterans of B Company fondly recalled their moment of glory at Big Creek Gap, the magnitude of the tiny skirmish growing with each telling.[6]

Two months before James Cooley reported to Charleston, John Condon was released from Federal prison as part of the Vicksburg exchange. The disabled Irishman returned home to Rogersville where he was happily reunited with his wife, Bridget, and four sons. A true Southern patriot, Condon followed the example of his friend, Cooley, and sent his oldest son to replace himself. In the summer of 1864 Private Michael L. Condon, age seventeen, reported as an aide to the quartermaster of Brigadier General John Crawford Vaughn's all East-Tennessee brigade of mounted infantry. The youthful Condon participated in the East Tennessee Mountain War at the Battles of Strawberry Plains and Bull's Gap. Following the war the Condons moved from Rogersville to Knoxville, where they established a prosperous railroad construction business. In 1884 thirty-seven-year-old Michael Condon, a native Virginian and a prominent Democrat, is believed to have been the first member of the Catholic faith to be elected to stateside office in Tennessee. He held the position of Railroad Commissioner until the system was federalized several years later. Today hundreds of living Americans are descended from Sergeant John Condon, B Company, Third Confederate Battalion, Engineer Corps, Department of East Tennessee—the vast majority of whom have never heard of him.[7]

NOTES

1. W. T. Houck. Military Service Records (MSR), National Archives and Records Administration (NARA), Confederate Record Group (RG) No. 109; James D. Porter, *Tennessee Confederate Military History: Tennessee* (Atlanta, 1899), p. 428.

2. J. Condon, T. F. Cooley, MSR, NARA, RG No. 109.

3. G. Margrave, L. A. McCauley. MSR, NARA, RG No. 109; Muster Rolls, "Third Confederate Battalion, Engineer Corps, Department of East Tennessee"; Porter, p. 430.

4. Ed Gleeson, "Sergeant John Condon: Tennessee Engineer," *Confederate Veteran* magazine (May–June 1991), p. 17.

5. Gleeson, p. 19; E. B. Long, *Civil War Day By Day: An Almanac, 1861–1865* (New York, 1971), p. 264; Muster Rolls; Porter, p. 428.

6. J. L. Cooley MSR, NARA, RG No. 109; Porter, p. 430.

7. Gleeson, p. 23; Horn, Stanley, ed., *Tennesseeans in the Civil War Civil War*, Centennial Commission (Nashville, 1964), vol. 1, pp. 298–305; Porter, p. 429.[Author's Note: John and Michael Condon were ancestors of the author.

INDEX

Harding, Mrs. Robert, 73
Harris, Brig. Gen. Nathaniel (CSV), 28, 31
Harris, Gov. Isham G., 83, 112
Harrison, Col. George P. (CSV), 15, 16
Hart, Lt. Col. Harrison E. (USV), 123, 129
Hatcher's Run, Battle of (First), 33
Hatcher's Run, Battle of (Second), 34–41
   casualties, 38
Hawley, Col. Joseph R. (USV), 14, 15
Haynie, Col. Isham (USV), 88
Heagney, Msgr. Harold J., 55
Healey, Capt. J. H. (CSV), 117
Heiman, Col. Adolphus (CSV), 86, 88, 90, 91, 92–93, 106
   death, 93
Henry, Col. Guy V. (USV), 13
Heth, Maj. Gen. Henry, 34
Higginson, Col. Thomas W. (USV), 10
Hill, Lt. Gen. A. Powell (CVS), 30, 33, 35
Hill, Gen. D. Harvey (CSV), 71
Hilton Head Island, SC, 12
Hoffman, Col. John S. (CSV), 35, 36
Hoke, Maj. Gen. Robert F. (CSV), 31
Hood, Maj. Gen. John Bell (CSV), 99, 103
Hopkins, Col. Charles F. (CSV), 7, 8, 26
Horn, Stanley F., 83
Horsehoe Ridge, Battle of, 101
Houck, Second Lt. William (CSV), 133, 134, 135, 136
Houghton, Henry, 61
Hubner, Charles W., 71
Humphreys, Maj. Gen. Andrew A. (USV), 34
Hunter's Farm, MO, 114, 115

Hyde, Sgt. James (CSV), 96

Iron Brigade, 33

Jackson, MS, 97
Jacksonville, FL, 6, 12, 17
Jayne, Col. Joseph M. (CSV), 33
Johnson, Maj. Gen. Bushrod R. (CSV), 87, 100
Johnson, Brig. Gen. Richard (USV), 102
Johnston, Gen. A. Sidney (CSV), 87, 113

Keegan, Capt. Patrick H. (USV), 102
Kelsey, 1st Lt. Theodore (CSV), 99
Kenrick, Bishop Peter Richard, 56
King, Col. J. Horace (CSV), 33
Ku Klux Klan, 67

Lafayette Road, 99, 100
Lake City, FL, 7
Lang, Col. David (CSV), 21, 23, 26, 40
Laser, Rabbi Abraham, 68
Laser, Rose, 68
Lauman, Col. Jacob G. (USV), 116, 117, 118, 121, 123, 129
Layton, Capt. J. D. (CSV), 117
Leahy, Pvt. David (CSV), 118
Lee and Gordon's Mills, Battle of, 99
Lee, Maj. Gen. Fitz (CSV), 28
Lee, Gen. Robert E., 5, 19, 29, 30, 34, 35, 67
   surrenders to Grant, 60
Lee, Lt. Gen. Stephen D. (CSV), 74, 103
Lincoln, President Abraham, 10, 12, 53, 57, 83
   assassinated, 60
Lipscomb, Msgr. Oscar H., 55